Brush Up on Your Hair Magick

Energy Brushing: There are many ways to raise magickal energy. One method is the act of brushing one's hair. It doesn't matter how long or short your hair is; if you can run a brush through it, you can brush up some major magickal energy for any imaginable need or desire. This is especially true on cold days when the brush will stir up static electricity and you can feel your hair crackle with a power all its own.

Brushing can be hard on your hair and, if done too often or with a rough hand, can cause breakage. Be gentle when you brush for magick. Brushing vigorously or quickly will not raise any more energy than will doing it slowly or gently.

As you brush, visualize any magickal need and, if you like, recite your words of power to help keep you focused. When you feel you have raised all the energy you can, put your brush down and run your hands over your hair to smooth it down. As you do this, visualize the energy built up in it being released toward your goal.

About the Author

Edain McCoy became a self-initiated Witch in 1981 and has been an active part of the Pagan community since her formal initiation into a large San Antonio coven in 1983. She has been researching alternative spiritualities since her teens, when she was first introduced to Kaballah, or Jewish mysticism. Since then she has studied a variety of magickal paths including Celtic Witchcraft, Appalachian folk magick, and Curanderismo, a Mexican-American folk tradition. Today she is part of the Wittan Irish Pagan tradition, where she is a priestess of Brighid and an elder. An alumnus of the University of Texas with a B.A. in History, she is active in several professional writer's organizations, is listed in the reference guide *Contemporary Authors,* and occasionally presents workshops on magickal topics or works individually with students who wish to study Witchcraft. This former woodwind player for the Lynchburg (VA) Symphony claims both the infamous feuding McCoy family of Kentucky and Sir Roger Williams, the seventeenth-century religious dissenter, as branches on her ethnically diverse family tree. In her "real life," Edain works as a licensed stockbroker.

To Write to the Author

If you wish to contact the author or would like more information about this book, please write to the author in care of Llewellyn Worldwide and we will forward your request. Both the author and publisher appreciate hearing from you and learning of your enjoyment of this book and how it has helped you. Llewellyn Worldwide cannot guarantee that every letter written to the author can be answered, but all will be forwarded. Please write to:

Edain McCoy
℅ Llewellyn Worldwide
P.O. Box 64383, Dept. 0-7387-0168-8
St. Paul, MN 55164-0383, U.S.A.

Please enclose a self-addressed stamped envelope for reply,
or $1.00 to cover costs. If outside U.S.A., enclose
international postal reply coupon.

Many of Llewellyn's authors have websites with additional information and resources. For more information, please visit our website at

http://www.llewellyn.com

Edain McCoy

Enchantments

200 Spells for Bath & Beauty Enhancement

2001
Llewellyn Publications
St. Paul, Minnesota 55164-0383, U.S.A.

FIRST EDITION
Second Printing, 2001

Book design and editing by Rebecca Zins
Cover art © Photodisc
Cover design by Lisa Novak

Library of Congress Cataloging-in-Publication Data
McCoy, Edain, 1957-
    Enchantments: 200 spells for bath & beauty enhancement / Edain McCoy.—1st ed.
       p.   cm.
    Includes bibliographical references (p.) and index.
    ISBN 0-7387-0168-8
    1. Magic. 2. Beauty, Personal—Miscellanea.   3. Women—Health and hygiene—Miscellanea. I. Title.

BF1623.B43 E64 2001
133.4'46—dc21

                                                  2001038024

Llewellyn Worldwide does not participate in, endorse, or have any authority or responsibility concerning private business transactions between our authors and the public.

    All mail addressed to the author is forwarded but the publisher cannot, unless specifically instructed by the author, give out an address or phone number.

    Any Internet references contained in this work are current at publication time, but the publisher cannot guarantee that a specific location will continue to be maintained. Please refer to the publisher's website for links to authors' websites and other sources.

Disclaimer: The spells in this book are to be undertaken at your own risk. The publisher and author assume no responsibility for actions occurring as a result of performing any spells in this book.

    Spells containing herbs are to be used with care, as some herbs may be dangerous for your health. Please check with a medical professional before ingesting or applying any herbs.

Llewellyn Publications
A Division of Llewellyn Worldwide, Ltd.
P.O. Box 64383, Dept. 0-7387-0168-8
St. Paul, MN 55164-0383, U.S.A.
www.llewellyn.com

 Printed in the United States of America on recycled paper

Other Books by Edain McCoy

Witta: An Irish Pagan Tradition

A Witch's Guide to Faery Folk

The Sabbats

How to Do Automatic Writing

Celtic Myth & Magick

Magick & Rituals of the Moon

Entering the Summerland

Inside a Witches' Coven

Making Magick

Mountain Magick

Celtic Women's Spirituality

Astral Projection for Beginners

Bewitchments

Ostara (February 2002)

for
Jack

who sees the beauty
my mirror misses

Contents

Four: Lotions and Potions . . . 69

Five: Hair Magick . . . 103

Six: Perfumes and Aromatherapy . . . 129

xiv

Eight: The Glamoury . . . 161

Warning

All of the ingredients in the recipes presented in this book are considered to be safe for general use in limited quantities. However, this margin of safety does not take into account substances that might not be suitable for women who are pregnant or nursing, for use on the very young or by the elderly, or which might produce severe allergic reactions in some sensitive individuals. Common sense should dictate that homemade cleansing or beauty products be guarded from children and pets with the same vigor as would commercially prepared products.

None of the recipes herein are to be taken internally or placed within any body orifice. They are meant for external, magickal, cosmetic use only. The reader is advised to test all ingredients for allergic reaction prior to general use, and to consult a qualified physician or botanist if preexisting medical conditions—particularly pregnancy—might contraindicate the use of any herbal recipe. Neither the author nor the publisher can be responsible for any misuse of or adverse reaction to any recipe presented in or suggested by this book.

Introduction
Beauty: The Image We Love to Hate

O beauty ever ancient and ever new! Too late
I loved you. And, behold, you were within me,
and I out of myself, and there I searched for you.
—St. Augustine

Human beings have been concerned about appearances ever since the first primitive man noticed his reflection in a pool of water and reached up a tentative hand to smooth his matted hair. From that point onward, cultural standards for beauty, some of them bizarre and some even harmful, have been held up to humanity as a measure of self-worth. This has been especially true for the world's women.

While modern feminism teaches us to eschew enhancing the body for the sake of appearance, modern Western culture and its power brokers have elevated the pursuit of beauty to a religious pilgrimage more persuasive than that of our most seductive cults. The combined beauty, diet, and fashion industry rakes in more than 100 billion dollars each year as it coerces women—and more and more men—to seek an idealized physical image that the vast majority can never attain. In the ultimate conflict of interest, those who stand to reap the greatest profit from the sale of those products also dictate the editorial content of the fashion magazines that are the beauty religion's bibles.

Does this mean that we must reject any beautification of the physical self in order to preserve our individualism? Of course not. A free-thinking individual makes these choices for herself. Rejecting our appearance would be just as detrimental to our sense of self-worth as would rejecting our intellect, our talents, our interests, our sexuality, or our dreams of success. Our appearance is part of who we are, and we must address it as we would any other aspect of ourselves or risk the mental and emotional illnesses brought on by the self-hatred that such denial produces.

The origins of the beauty quest may not be as insidious as we have been taught to believe. The facial makeup that Western women consider their gender's private province is and has been worn in all cultures by members of both sexes to do no more than make the body attractive by whatever cultural standard is used as a measurement. Makeup has also served important spiritual functions, first appearing as a ritual tool similar to masking. It allowed the wearer to transform himself or herself into another being, and to use that as a vehicle to travel to other realms of existence, to return with benefits for the community. This impulse remains a strong but unconscious undertow in our quest for physical attractiveness.

Masking has practical applications in everyday situations as well. A woman standing alone in front of a mirror may find she enjoys applying color to her face just to see what transformations are possible—just because it's fun. It may also be functional. She may be using a flesh-toned foundation to cover a scar from surgery or to disguise a burn mark, or she may just feel like looking a little more dramatic that day. She may be using mascara to help her look more alert for an important meeting when she's been unable to sleep the night before. Or she may avoid makeup altogether and exercise her right to show the world the face the Goddess gave her at birth.

In recent years anthropologists have hypothesized that the beauty quest may be hard to set aside because its pursuit is encoded in our genes. This theory states that many of the characteristics we view as beautiful are really hallmarks of fertility, and that our attraction to these features is an impulse directed by the most basic instinct of all life: to reproduce. Broad-shouldered men with narrow hips, women with small waists and curvaceous hips, large female breasts, and symmetrical facial features may all be interpreted as fertility signals that trigger this primitive mating response within us. They may also be the root cause of our mania for the cult of youth that seems to grow stronger with each passing generation. It's a biological fact. Young people are the most fertile.

Beholding beauty may also be part of our process of spiritual evolution. An old proverb teaches us that a thing of beauty is a joy forever. James Redfield, author of a popular book on New Age spirituality, *The Celestine Prophecy*, states that the more beauty we can see, the more we are able to evolve. He also advocates the giving and receiving of beautiful things to achieve inner peace and mutual understanding.

On whichever side of the beauty argument one sides, the fact remains that the need to feel physically attractive is just as important to our sense of wholeness and self-worth as are our senses of belonging, intellect, acceptance, and our sense of connection to a higher power. This is clear by the way our children react to beauty's lure. Little girls whose academic achievements and talents are lauded at the expense of telling her she is also attractive end up with just as much damage to their self-esteem as those who are taught their only value is in their appearance. The appearance pressure is affecting boys, too. By the onset of puberty, boys who feel their bodies are lacking physical appeal often develop perfectionist ideals for other areas of their lives that are just as impossible to meet as the appearance standard. No human is just a body or just a brain, and to try and make us so is to irreparably lessen us by limiting our choices of what constitutes wholeness and self-value to us as individuals.

The Face of Ambivalence

Beauty is the image we love to hate. We are conscious of, yet loathe the fact, that our sense of power or weakness is directly connected to our sense of how we look at any given time. Even worse, it relates to how we feel we look at any given time in relation to those around us. A woman who feels she looks the fattest, thinnest, tallest, shortest, darkest, palest, best-looking, or worst-looking in a room has those feelings reflected in how she interacts with others. Some women go so far as to avoid social situations altogether when they've gained a little weight or if they have a blemish on their face.

Rather than realize that our beauty rituals can be turned into personal pampering time, ones in which magick is inherent and just waiting to be tapped, we may dread them as chores, more convinced of their failure than their success. It doesn't help that some of history's most beautiful women have been considered "bad girls." Some of them have been linked with beauty rituals so bizarre that they wouldn't be believed in today's cynical world. Yet we take these old stories as facts rather than with the proverbial grain of salt we would swallow with any other political pundits. Did Marie Antoinette really bathe in milk to stay pale and soft? Did Lucrezia Borgia really wash her face in the blood of children to remain youthful? Did Cleopatra, one of the world's most powerful rulers, really have as much time each day to devote to her appearance as legend claims? Did Russia's Catherine the Great really mate with horses because no man could satisfy her profound lust?

Because much of extant mythology was codified after the period of patriarchal rule took hold, our myths underscore our ambivalent feelings toward beauty's pursuit by showing us conflicting imagery of beauty that both lauds and lowers women. Just as in today's workplace, they show that women cannot win this war; not with men and not with each other. If they are beautiful, they are dangerous. If they are not beautiful, they have no value. If they strive for beauty, they are vain or allied with evil forces. If they eschew beauty, they are dangerous harridans who hate men. In general, we can divide mythic beauties into eight distinct categories.

The Tragic Beauty

Beauty is often shown as being its own downfall, as in the legend of Ireland's Deirdre, whose choice of the man she loves leads her nation to war when a king feels he should be the man to wed the great beauty.

The Deadly Beauty

Many myths and folk legends show beauty as being dangerous to men, as exemplified in Germany's Lorelei of the Rhine River, the faery spirit who lures sailors to their deaths on the rocky banks. Other legends tell of beautiful female creatures who lure men to water to drown them, such as the white ladies of Europe's seacoasts.

The Plundered Beauty

Beauty can be a danger to women, as shown in the semihistorical legends of the mass abduction and rape of the Sabine women in ancient Rome. This same rationale—that beauty is to be punished for its seductiveness—is used today to justify much violence against women.

The Imprisoned Beauty

Beauty can be jealously guarded, such as in the faery tale of Rapunzel, the beautiful, long-haired princess locked in an inaccessible tower for fear that her beauty would either lead her to mate with the wrong man or supplant her mother in her father's affections. It is also seen in Greek mythology in the story of the lonely but adored Psyche, who is kept isolated in darkness by her lover Eros, who wishes to guard her affections for himself.

The Devouring Beauty

This is the beauty of the most powerful Goddess; an ugly, dark beauty that is both repugnant and compelling, as in the old Halloween Witch. This devourer consumes all who love her too much. She is demanding and always seeking more. She is the personification of the bottomless pit of the insatiable female appetite, as is seen in India's Kali and the Irish death and war Triple Goddess, the Morrighan.

The Enchanted Beauty

This ephemeral beauty is apt to either hide her true face or to pose so many faces that no one can determine her true appearance or know when it will change again. This is exemplified in the legend of Ireland's Niall of the Nine Hostages, whose riding party is stopped by an elderly woman whom they find unattractive and who challenges the men to dismount and kiss her. Niall alone braved the challenge, and the woman turned into a beautiful young princess. In myths such as these the women is the personification of sovereignty, who bestows on kings the right to rule her land.

The Created Beauty

Myths also tell us of beautiful women created at the hands of men, such as Greece's Pygmalion or Wales's Blodeuwedd. Both were creations of men who then fell in love with what they believed to be their ideal females. Both creations proved to have minds of their own and, eventually, both rejected their creators and chose their own mates.

The Lost Beauty

This is the hag, the crone, whose days of beauty by society's standard are behind her. She is not viewed as possessing either inner or outer beauty now that she is older and perceived as jealous of young beauty, which she will destroy if she can. This is seen both in the Halloween Witch and in the faery tale of Snow White, wherein the wicked stepmother seeks to murder her young stepdaughter for being deemed more beautiful than she.

With images like these helping to pull us both ways in the beauty argument, it's no wonder modern women run scared to the beauty counter—damned if they do and damned if they don't.

Beauty Rituals

Spells and magick using beauty rituals are ancient. Magick using perfumes, shampoos, hair brushes, mirrors, lotions, soaps, masks, and face coloring have been practiced since before recorded history, mostly—but not exclusively—by women. These spells not only sought beauty, they also paved the way for love, conferred protection, purified the spirit, enhanced fertility, opened the psychic senses, and prepared the women for sacred ritual in which they became Goddess.

The Goddess in her many forms, from thin to fat and from old to young, was the standard for female beauty in many ancient societies. When women "made up" to invoke her spirit into their own, they too became divine. The modern English word "beauty" comes from the Latin *beatus*, meaning "blessed," a term no longer applied to those who seek to become Goddesslike through their appearance, but to those who were born "lucky," blessed with the genetic ability to achieve the nearly impossible beauty standards of our modern Western culture.

This book does not advocate any single beauty standard, but recognizes the right of all people to be who they are and to do with their bodies and faces whatever they choose within the tenet of "As it harms none, do what you will." This book will not show you how to put on makeup. The idea that there exists one makeup style that fits all faces is as silly as saying there is one dress style that flatters and suits all women. This book also does not advocate the wearing of makeup to be considered attractive or to achieve the best results of any spell.

Any appearance-related choice you make should be made from knowledge about yourself and the culture in which you live, and should suit your needs and desires. Do you really feel better ten pounds thinner or do you just think you do because it is a weight goal closer to the cultural standard? Do you really wear mascara to look alert or do you feel you just aren't pretty enough without it? Do you wear lipstick because you like it or because all your friends do? The spells in this book are intended to help you turn the beauty rituals already in place in your life into moments of magick that can transform your life and make of it what you want.

You'll find the recipes are not about makeup, other than one or two used in a ritual context. They use magickally empowered soaps, shampoos, and other daily hygiene and skin care products as catalysts for magick. You gotta bathe anyway, right? Why not turn that time into magick?

Using daily rituals for magick is common practice. We use other daily routines to help feed magickal needs all the time. We use the rhythm of our footsteps to focus, we use household tasks to do psychic cleansing, and we use that cup of herbal tea at bedtime to ensure restful sleep and pleasant dreams. The events that take place behind the closed door of your bathroom have been used similarly for thousands of years to achieve magickal goals. If you're seeking time for magick in your busy life, it makes sense that you don't need a book teaching you how to be beautiful but to help you take those beauty rituals you already have in place and use them to make magick. We have to wash our hair anyway, so why not create our own shampoos with magickal ingredients and turn that chore into a ritual?

Enchantment's eight chapters are rooted in the concept of beauty as being yourself and liking yourself. Magick won't work without self-confidence. Beauty already exists in each of us as daughters of the Goddess. If we do nothing else in our magickal lives we should reclaim that conviction and embrace it without doubt, in spite of the media images that tell us we can't do this because we're somehow lacking if we don't purchase and use the latest overpriced fad beauty product. The Goddess gives us her face, her body, and her spirit. It is holy and sacred and full of the power of magickal potential waiting to be unleashed.

one
The Ingredients

Where is the love, beauty
and truth we seek,
But in our minds?
—Percy Bysshe Shelley

The ingredients used for the magickal recipes in this book use many lotion and soap bases to which fresh or dried herbs, or essential or cold-pressed oils, have been added. Essential or aromatic oils are the volatile distilled plant extracts often sold as perfumes. Cold-pressed oils are fatty oils, such as olive or nut oils, that are usually used as a base for essential oil blends.

If you grow or purchase fresh herbs, you can preserve them by drying them. This is best accomplished by hanging them on a drying rack in a warm, dry place for six to eight weeks. You can create the perfect drying rack from the sweater-drying racks found in discount department stores.

Avoid using synthetic ingredients in magickal preparations, especially your essential oils. Perfumed or scented oils are created without natural ingredients. Natural ingredients work best in magick because their energies are in harmony with the magickal goals we seek and they contain the correct energies to act as catalysts to help us make our magick work. They resonate with the power of the Mother Earth in which they were grown and their energy patterns and precise scent—both of which are needed for your best spellwork—cannot be duplicated.

The herbs and oils selected for the recipes in this book are a combination of those known to have cosmetic effects on the skin or hair or that act as catalysts to help you achieve specific magickal goals. This chapter will explain some of those ingredients so that you will better be able to see how these recipes were created, and so you can begin to craft your own magickal bath and beauty spells for any need.

Herbs, oils, and other natural substances have a long history of use in magick. Their natural energies have been experimented with for so many centuries that those who practice magickal arts know almost intuitively what plants correspond best to energies of what magickal need. Always remember that *the magick is not in the herb, but in you.* The herb acts as a catalyst to help you focus your energy and, because it contains sympathetic energy, it helps you channel that energy toward its goal.

In some cases, the scent of the herb alone is all it will take to trigger the magick. This is known in popular culture as aromatherapy. Aromatherapy is gaining acceptance within the most mainstream circles since it has been "discovered" that lavender is calming, lemon is invigorating, jasmine is seductive, and so on. Magickal people have known these scent tricks for eons. Aroma magick is created each time you use a particular scent or scent blend for a particular spell. Over time, just a whiff of the scent is enough to trigger your magickal mind to action. This is the basis for some very strong magick. I know that just the slightest whiff of sandalwood oil mentally transports me back to one of my earliest and happiest times in magick, and it puts me in the right frame of mind for crafting successful spells.

All the recipes contained in this book are meant strictly for external, cosmetic, and magickal use and should never be ingested or placed in any body cavity.

Most of the ingredients used are considered to be safe for general use in limited quantities. Be aware that some herbal concentrations are able to penetrate the skin and be absorbed into the body. Therefore, most of the recipes in the book are not suitable for women who are pregnant or nursing. They should also not be used on young children or on the elderly.

Many people choose herbal health and skin care products under the mistaken assumption that "natural" means "100 percent free of side effects." Wise herbalists never forget that plants were our first medicines and that many of today's miracle drugs were derived from plants. All living things have a chemical make-up that, when mixed with our own chemistry, may not peacefully coexist. Herbal side effects can be just as severe and just as deadly as those of any prescription drug. Use all herbal preparations with caution, even those not taken internally.

Having a regulating authority declare an herb generally safe, such as is done by the United States Food and Drug Administration, does not mean that substance will not cause an allergic reaction in certain sensitive individuals. You should do an allergy test prior to using any herb as a cosmetic. Do this by crushing some of the herb and placing it under a bandage against the skin on the inside of your arm, just below the elbow fold. The same should be done for oils and other substances. Leave this in place for twenty-four hours, or until an adverse reaction occurs. If twenty-four hours pass with no itching, swelling, or redness, you probably will not have any problems using that substance. Treat any reaction as you normally would, with topical or oral antihistamines or, if the situation merits, seek emergency medical help. Also remember that allergies can develop at any time during your life and can even cause a substance you've used for years to suddenly become potentially dangerous to you.

Don't be tempted to pick your own wild herbs unless you are an expert botanist. Many plants are easily confused, even by the pros, and Mother Nature has protected her babies by having the most poisonous plants masquerade as some of the most benign. There are so many reputable dealers who sell inexpensive dried herbs and plants that taking risks is pointless. Look to your local occult bookstore for assistance or check out Appendix A in the back of this book for a list of mail-order resources.

The Major Ingredients

Almond Oil

A low-scent oil often used as a base for essential oil blends, almond oil is very hydrating and often found in high-quality moisturizers. Almonds are used in spells for fertility, grounding, beauty, love, and prosperity. Do not be tempted to substitute peanut oil for almond oil. Peanut oil is a common cooking oil and, like most cooking oils, is a fatty oil derived from a cold-pressed process. It is not an essence and is not hydrating. Peanuts are also common allergens that produce dangerous reactions in many people, especially children.

•Aloe Vera

This is a popular ingredient in skin lotions. The gel that comes from a broken aloe leaf can be used to help soothe and heal burns. In magick, aloe vera is used for spells of protection, wealth, and beauty. Keep refrigerated.

Apple

Apples are used in love magick, in rites to honor ancestors and call spirits, and in spells to honor the Goddess. Apples can be puréed in a blender and added to magickal formulas that produce a mild astringent effect. Apple blossom is a sweet scent sometimes used in love or beauty spells.

Anise

Used as a hair rinse for darker hair, anise is also popular in spells to create lust and passion and to enhance psychic energy. Don't confuse anise with licorice, though; they are not the same thing.

Castile Soap

This is an olive oil soap first produced in the Castile region of Spain in the thirteenth century. It is easily grated and melted to make other solid soaps and provides a low-scent base for magickal soap products using essential oils. Castile soap is very mild and nonastringent. It also comes in a liquid form that makes the perfect base for shampoos and gel soaps, though it may be too hydrating for oily hair. A note to vegetarians or those who eschew animal products: Some castiles include animal fat, which originally gave the olive oil soap the fatty acids it needed to give it its cleaning power. Today some of these still contain lard, but most use vegetable oils, so check your ingredients list carefully when purchasing castile soaps at drug stores or by mail order.

Chamomile

This is used in spells for relaxation and is often found in herbal hair preparations, especially for blondes. Avoid using chamomile if you are allergic to ragweed. They come from the same plant family, so people sensitive to ragweed may have an unpleasant reaction to chamomile.

Cinnamon

This spicy herb is used frequently in spells for lust and protection. The oil is very irritating to the skin.

Clay

Our grandmothers tried to tell us about this one. Clay is a great skin softener and makes an excellent facial mask for extracting dirt and oil. Don't use clay straight from your backyard, which has too much dirt and trace minerals. Pure clay is cheap and worth the purchase.

Clove

Clove oil is a rich scent, but is toxic and can irritate the skin, so use it with caution. Clove is often added to spells for protection and warding and makes a great catalyst to halt gossip.

Eucalyptus

This oil is reputed to have natural antibiotic and antiviral properties. Not surprisingly, it is used primarily in spells for healing and health.

Glycerin

The hydrating and moisture-retaining substance we know as glycerin is actually a byproduct of soap processing. This complex process is not covered in this book, but the byproduct is recommended in several of the skin lotion recipes. Bottles of glycerin can be purchased inexpensively in most drug stores.

Honey

Honey and the bees who create it are sacred to many of the world's Gods and Goddesses. Honey appears in spells ancient and modern as a catalyst for love, beauty, and health. It is also used in medicinal preparations and in skin care products.

Jasmine

Jasmine is actually the general name for over two hundred species of tropical shrubs. The one we use for perfume is from a vine with waxy white foliage that has an exotic and sensual quality. It makes a fine oil or incense, or can be used dried. It is used in magick for prophetic dreams, psychic powers, and love and romance.

Jojoba Oil

Used to add shine and moisture to the hair and scalp, jojoba oil has properties similar to collagen, the elastic in your skin, that can help strengthen the skin and may have some beneficial effect on hair follicles.

Lavender

The soft, feminine scent of lavender releases chemicals in the brain that produce a feeling of relaxation. In magick it is used widely in spells for love, sleep, romance, and peace. Classicists tell us lavender oil was added to the waters of the famous Roman baths to cleanse both the body and the spirit. It was also used as a perfume in ancient Egypt.

Lemon

The scent of lemon is invigorating and stimulates the intellect. Lemon is used in spells for protection, courage, and strength. It is a mild astringent with bleaching properties that is often found in hair washes for fair-haired people.

Lime

Lime protects and is used in spells for exorcism.

Lilac Oil

Lilac oil is soothing to the spirit and is used to induce visions of past lives.

Lotus

Lotus is a sensual floral scent with Asian overtones. The oil is most often used in spells for sleep, peace, and love.

Maidenhair

Sacred to Goddesses of beauty, this is used in spells for drawing love and enhancing appearance.

Myrtle

Myrtle is a mild astringent and popular herb in love spells in England and the American South.

Oatmeal

Oatmeal makes an excellent skin softener and facial mask.

Olive Oil

This cold-pressed oil is a favorite as a base for making other oil blends. Alone, it is used in magick for purification, love, and peace.

Orange

The scent of orange is invigorating and helps settle a distracted mind. It is related to the sun, friendships, personal attraction, and used in spells for money, protection, and attracting friends. Orange oil has found a new incarnation in commercial products to clean and to keep parasites off pets.

Parsley

A simple breath freshener and diuretic, parsley is used in spells to aid in astral projection or create the illusion of invisibility.

Rose

The sweet scent of rose has so long been associated with romance that our minds are immediately triggered in that direction when we catch a whiff. Its primary use in magick is in love spells, but it can also be used in spells for beauty and healing.

Rosemary

Rosemary smells clean and clear. It is so versatile that it is the one herb no magickal practitioner—or good cook—should be without. Rosemary is used in spells for lust, love, memory, healing, mental prowess, vigor, exorcism, and purification.

Safflower Oil

This is another low-scent oil that makes a good base for creating oil blends.

Salts

Salts include Epsom salts, table salts, sea salt, and baking soda. They are used in preparations to soften and exfoliate the skin. Magickally, they are used for grounding, protection, and to banish negativity.

Sandalwood

Sandalwood smells woodsy and exotic. It is used in magick for purification, peace, healing, and love, and is often included in spells connected with moon or mirror magick.

Vervain

Vervain is a popular herb in love spells.

Vinegar

The high acid content of vinegars helps remove dead skin cells from the surface layer of the skin, a process known as exfoliation. It makes a nice astringent and adds shine to hair. Use apple cider vinegar for best results. Vinegar is also used in spells for protection, banishing, and turning back negative magick.

Water

It almost goes without saying that water will be a component of most any bath and beauty preparation you make. While tap water is fine for bath magick, use spring water if possible to add to your magickal preparations. Avoid distilled water that has had the magickal essence of its elements distorted through processing.

Yarrow

Used heavily in love spells and spells for courage and banishment of negativity.

Magick: The Cohesive Ingredient

Mixing up some exotic herbs and oils and uttering a few lines from a book will not make magick work. It's just not that simple. If it were, everyone would be beautiful, rich, famous, and have everything they ever want within arm's reach. Those who practice magick or who follow magickal religions will tell you that spellcrafting is work. Hard work. It requires physical, emotional, and mental effort, not once, but over and over.

This chapter cannot hope to replace an entire text on natural magickal practices. If you are a newcomer to the magickal arts, it is recommended that you seek out at least one of these books and learn and practice the exercises presented to you. Among the books available right now are Amber K's *True Magick* (Llewellyn, 1992), Doreen Valiente's *Natural Magick* (Phoenix, 1988), Marion Weinstein's *Positive Magic* (Phoenix, 1983), Raven Grimassi's *Wiccan Magick* (Llewellyn, 1998), and my own *Making Magick* (Llewellyn, 1997).

There are some universally recognized steps used to create successful spells. Most long-time practitioners add some steps of their own but, for all practical purposes, they remain the same from magician to magician, tradition to tradition, and from past to present.

Desire and need

Strong emotional involvement

Knowledge and realistic expectations

Conviction and faith

The ability to keep silent

Pursuing the goal in the physical world

These six steps have several variations, but they lie at the heart of successful magick and feed naturally off one another. Think about how one is linked to another like threads on a web. Without a desire born of need there can be no emotional involvement. Without emotional involvement there can be no desire to drive the spell. Desire without the knowledge to do the spell is useless, and knowledge without faith in the outcome will negate any effort. Keeping silent to prevent losing the power you're putting into the spell is essential for helping you to pursue your goal in the physical world and not just relying on magick to do everything for you.

Remember that successful spellcrafting requires your input on all levels of your being. If you are trying to take an unformed idea and manifest it in the physical world, then also working for it in both the unformed and physical worlds makes sense. This daily pursuit of your goal helps reinforce your desire, and so the cycle starts all over again, one step feeding into the next.

Almost any spell will require you to have basic magickal skills. Don't panic if you don't have them yet. The ability to make magick lies within all of us, though you may have to work to fully develop your personal power to a place where magick comes more easily. When doing the spells in this book, or any other, you will need to use the following skills:

Visualization

This is the art of "seeing" the spell's goal in your mind in vivid detail. Doing this helps empower the image by linking its unseen-world form to you in the physical world. This allows it to gain in density and, eventually, manifest. Visualization is the conscious mind's way of letting the subconscious and superconscious minds know exactly what you expect from them by pulling them into alignment.

Visualization is arguably the most important step in the magickal process and should not be skimped on. Plan this step as carefully as you would your catalysts, words, or gestures to make sure you are asking for precisely what you want.

Centering and Balancing

This is the art of pulling deep into your center all your energies and any surrounding energies so you can mold them to your will and send them out to do your will. You must feel calm, at your center point, and in harmony with the inner and outer worlds to best connect your magick to all these realms. This is the "magickal mindset" mentioned earlier that is necessary to trigger a magickal response on all levels of your being.

Raising and Sending Magickal Energy

This is the ability to build on those collected energies and, when they reach their peak, to mentally and physically will them to travel where they need to go to work best for you. This is done by chanting, drumming, dancing, and building or drawing in the earth's energy, then mentally releasing it toward its goal when ready. Visualization is important to making this step successful.

Empowering, Charging, or Enchanting

These three terms are used interchangeably to refer to the same process. Objects or magickal tools contain no power in and of themselves. They may share affinities and share a long history of being used for specific types of magick, but the power that drives them comes from the one who enacts the spell. Energy pertaining to the goal must be channeled into those catalysts to help them work for you.

Objects must first be clear of previous programming, which can occur without magickal intent. Do you remember when you believed you could catch someone's "cooties" merely by touching an object that had been touched by them? This is the result of their previous programming, the energy transfer that occurs when an object is handled and mentally interacted with. Objects absorb the energy of their owners. The more they are touched and thought about, the more energy they absorb. Place the object on the ground or hold it under running water while using visualization to clear it of its past programming.

The word "empowering" will be used a lot throughout this book for the sake of clarity. It refers to programming an object or catalyst with your magickal will rather than allowing random energies to accumulate. To give a catalyst your cooties, hold it, fondle it, and breathe on it, all the while mentally projecting into it your magickal desire. Visualization is, again, the key to making this skill work for you. Empowering is what makes any object a good conduit for helping channel the energy of your spell.

Altering Consciousness

This used to be a catchword in the 1970s before it fell from fashion. No matter what you choose to call it now, it is still very much a part of successful magick. Synonymous terms are going down, counting down, meditative state of mind, magickal mindset, magickal state of consciousness, receptive state, hypnogogic state, daydream state, alpha level, and slowed consciousness.

Altering consciousness is the art of being able to change the focus of your mind, to slow its pattern of energy so that it connects you to all other worlds and beings. You do this naturally when you read, sleep, or concentrate. Begin to experiment with meditation—simply holding single thoughts or mental pictures—for longer and longer periods of time to increase your ability to alter your consciousness at will.

Grounding

This is the essential last step in magick that helps us to take excess energy at the end of a spell and channel it safely away where it cannot be scattered or cause us to feel frazzled. Grounding also allows you to regain your normal waking consciousness and fully reenter the everyday world once more.

You can mentally channel unused magickal energy into Mother Earth or you may place your hands or feet under running water. Many practitioners choose to place their palms down flat on the ground after magick to ground themselves. Advanced magicians can ground themselves through visualization alone, a wonderful skill to cultivate for making magick in full view of the whole world while making sure no one knows but you.

Words of Power

The concept of using words of power has received so much attention over the past twenty years that it almost requires its own chapter to fully explain how it works. This is where a good text or two on basic magickal practice is invaluable. To be successful in magick you need that foundation and innate understanding, just as a concert pianist needs to practice scales over and over before being able to play a Beethoven sonata.

Like herbs, oils, candles, and other catalysts, the true magick of your spell is not in your words. They act as a conduit, a catalyst, for channeling your visualization and connecting your energies to the unseen or astral world where all magick begins the process of manifestation. Merely reciting a set of words over a spell will not make this happen.

Yet no one would deny that words are powerful when used with intent. Individually and in combination they evoke specific imagery in our minds. Once uttered where they can be heard by any other being, they can never be taken back completely. They reverberate forever, imprinting your will on the unseen. Once spoken, they have already set ideas and energies in motion that will eventually work their way back to you for good or bad.

Some of the images that words conjure up for us are archetypal or universal, and others are perceived by us in unique ways based on our own personal histories. Because of this they can help clarify both your intent and the visualization process, which is so vital to successful spellcrafting. When recited over and over with the full thrust of magickal will behind them, they reverberate over the universe and create energy patterns that—for better or worse—will eventually return to you as a completed action. This is why misspoken words have been regarded by folklore as dangerous. During the infamous Witch trials of Salem, Massachusetts, in 1692, words once spoken in innocence were used against the accused. For example, if someone said, "Better wear a hat or you'll get sick," and the person addressed fell ill, the colonists believed that proved the speaker had worked magick.

There are very few traditional words of power, also known as chants or charms. The traditional ones are usually identifiable by their archaic language, such as the use of "so mote it be" for "so it must be." However, obsolete language does not make one spell better than another. In fact, if you're really not clear on what those old words mean, your mind will not be able to latch onto them and use them to help produce the mental images necessary to make your spell work.

When chanted over and over, your words of power work like a mantra, a phrase designed to change the consciousness and its perception of reality. This is the essence of the magickal process and, in this respect, words are invaluable. Such words are usually created as couplets or quatrains, or sometimes even a series of quatrains that rhyme. This is partly because rhymes are easier to remember than standard prose and because reciting rhyming words provokes us to speak in rhythm, which further affects our consciousness and helps take it where we want it to go.

This is why repetitive words are so important in ritual. Ritual is nothing more than using standard patterns to change the direction of all levels of our consciousness. All spiritual practices employ this technique for helping adherents connect with the Godforce.

If you are interested in pursuing a study of magickal words, there are many sources where you can turn. The Judeo-Gnostic spiritual study known as Kaballah has a substudy of magickal words known as *gematria*. Gematria combines ancient alphabets, numerology, and word etymology to come up with some fascinating associations that can make each word you speak in any setting work most effectively. The Kaballistic text known as the *Zohar* has many legends about alphabet order and how the universe was created by no more magick than the uttering of words of power.

When creating the wording for any spell, or when altering the words in a spell you find in this book or any other, think carefully about your intent. Keep in mind that words are not necessary for all spells, and many spells in this book do not have any. However, words of power can always be added to any spell. Use the chants in this or any other books of spells as a model if you're unsure of how they should sound. Consider every single word and its impact on your mind. Make each word clear and precise but don't be afraid of them. We all have to learn our lessons by making magickal boo-boos before we can be fully successful. Almost any magickal practitioner can tell you tales of trying to manifest a car and ending up with a toy model or asking for someone to love them and receiving a pet dog.

My best words of power boo-boo came many years after I thought I'd learned all my lessons about what I said in spells. I created a glamoury spell (see chapter 8) to enhance my appearance and, among the sentences, there was one that began with the benign-sounding words "youthful face." I spent nearly two months battling teenage-style acne before it dawned on me what the problem was. I changed the youthful face line and the acne went away.

We all have an area of magick in which we excel, and some practitioners find they have an affinity for magickal words. If you are one of these people, you might want to make words your primary catalyst and create story spells or write lyrics for song spells that you use to weave your spells into being.

Magickal Ethics . . . Again

Please feel free to skip over this section if you've been practicing positive magick for awhile or have already learned the harsh lessons of using negative magick. So much has been written about magickal ethics that it almost seems redundant to have yet another discussion. But because this book does not take the paternal attitude that people must be sheltered from the negative aspects of magick, the discussion cannot be avoided. The laws of responsibility dictate that this material be presented just in case someone reading this is considering crossing that murky gray line for the first time.

In spite of the fact that magical practitioners are well aware of the serious repercussions of using harmful or manipulative magick, those types of spells are part of our magickal heritage, and so they appear in this book. The choice to use them or not is always that of the one who enacts the spell. A negative spell can be reworked to have no harmful side effects, and vice versa. The path of magick is, above all, one for the fully self-responsible. You can never blame the spell itself for any harm done.

The fast-growing religion of Witchcraft, which is based on the earliest religions of western Europe, is a magickal religion and, as such, teaches ethics to its initiates. They provide an excellent example of magickal laws because they are expoused frequently. The Craft has few laws but does adhere to its Rede, "As it harms none, do what you will." The real power of this law is that it is echoed in virtually all spiritual systems and religions throughout place and time. Obviously someone knows something here. What you do *will* come back to you. Period. Our ancestors found this out and created these ethics to help keep us from learning the hard way, like they did. Use caution in all you think, say, and do.

Think of the universe as a huge wheel that perpetually rotates around you. Energy you put onto the wheel goes out to the wheel's apex, then begins to circle back around to you. It brings with it not only your input onto it, but everyone else's as well. This is why it is so important to make completely sure you are not harming, manipulating, or in any way disregarding the free will and innate rights to any being's person, space, thoughts, or property. This is especially true in magick, where the thought process is concentrated and deliberate and, therefore, magnified.

This is also why it is best to keep silent as much as possible about your magickal goals. Even someone who does not practice magick or who steadfastly does not believe in it can produce energy that could counter the efforts of your spell, should they have an interest in preventing your goal from taking place. Sometimes simple jealousy is the culprit, even from the most well-meaning of friends.

Lastly, there are two arguments for negative magick that never hold up and always backfire. Don't be taken in by them. First of all, don't delude yourself that magick you're doing for some else's "own good" will bring you back positive results simply because you have good intentions. You are manipulating, and that is causing harm. It will only bring back to you a threefold smack of interference in your own free will. Secondly, don't think that firing off random magick with the claim that you do not believe in or accept a spiritual system to govern you will absolve you from responsibility. To say you do not believe in the mechanism that brings back to you that energy you send out is to say you do not believe in the very mechanism that makes magick work in the first place. Either the wheel turns or it doesn't. If it does, you cannot pick and choose which energy gets on board. You can't have it both ways. It may sound like a Catch-22 but it's one of the great mysteries magicians are always clamoring to know. This one is not hard to grasp. As Nin-Si-Ana, a priestess friend of mine, is fond of saying, "Well, just whack me upside the head with the frying pan of enlightenment!"

The world of magick is the heritage of humanity and belongs to no one individual or magickal tradition. It is there to assist all of us. Like any natural resource we must use it wisely and well and it will reward us ten times over for our efforts.

There are two methods often employed in spellcraft to attempt to overcome any unanticipated negative effects of a spell. One is to do some form of divination beforehand, such as reading the tarot cards or runes, to search for any unexpected magickal side effects. The other is to add words of power to your spell such as "as it harms none" or "as all will it to be" or "with goodwill toward all." This is then backed up with visualization that seeks contentment for all beings of all worlds who may be touched in any way by the energies of the spell you wish to do.

Bringing the Ingredients Together

There are several ways to process the herbal concoctions that will be used in this book, depending on how they are to be used. All should be created using the magickal principles just discussed if you wish to achieve the best effect. Good magickal recipes, like good magick itself, sometimes take time to produce. Certain types of herbal preparations can't be made in a day but they are worth the wait.

Keep in mind that from the time you decide to enact a spell, everything you do toward that spell is part of the magick: the preparation, the gathering of catalysts, the empowerment, the selection of words, the divination beforehand, the imagining, etc. Put your best magickal efforts behind every moment of your spell's creation and it will be strong.

You can buy most herbs in dried or ground form but if you like the process of pulverizing your own you might want to invest in a good old-fashioned mortar and pestle to grind your herbs by hand. This is a time-consuming process but it offers a great opportunity for you to put more magickal energy into the spell. The mortar and pestle makes us think of old-time Witches and alchemists and gives us a psychological boost where making magick is concerned.

Some modern magickal practitioners use the choppers, grinders, and food processors that are part of the standard kitchen wares of today. Certainly their magick is not harmed by these devices, but they are probably not helped either. The choice is yours to make, but it's recommended that you experiment with preparation methods at some point just to see how much, if any, difference using these modern appliances makes to your spells.

Be sure to label all your bottles and jars as you prepare specific types of bases to make your herbal magickal products, whether they contain individual herbal preparations or mixtures. Don't rely on scent or sight to tell you what is what because the human sense of smell just isn't that accurate and the jars may all start to look alike after a few weeks.

There are five types of herbal preparations you will need to know how to prepare. From these bases you can make almost any spell or magickal recipe, including the lotions, soaps, ointments, shampoos, and bath preparations described in this book.

Dry Herbal Blends

A dry herbal blend requires only the combining of dried herbs. These can be crumbled or powdered, depending on the recipe into which they will go. They can be ground together for a specific recipe or ground individually and then blended. The empowering process is still important to making them work the way you want. They should be blended with plenty of visualization to infuse them with your magickal intent.

Decoctions

A decoction is among the simplest forms of herbal preparations, probably one you're already using in your spellcraft. This requires only boiling an herb or combination of herbs. This can be done in a tea ball, or the mixture can be strained through cheesecloth or a very small colander to extract the herbal juices without retaining the herbs themselves.

Use a funnel to channel these into a storage container. Glass bottles with tight caps or stoppers are best. Decoctions keep fresh only a day or two, but you can stretch their life by several days by storing them in the refrigerator.

Infusions

An infusion is similar to a decoction but does not produce as much concentrated effect and is used frequently in magickal bath preparations. An infusion is synonymous with a tea or, in Witches' language, a potion.

To make an infusion, place dried herbs into a tea ball or cheesecloth, and place it in a tea cup, saucepan, or bath tub. Allow the herbs to gently infuse the surrounding water with their energies. Practitioners of medicinal herbalism use this process for making healing teas. An infusion produces the weakest liquid form of the herb. Use infusions immediately.

Tinctures

A tincture creates the strongest liquid form of the herb, with the exception of an essential oil. To make a tincture, you will need a grain alcohol, such as vodka, and a glass bottle with a tight seal for each tincture you wish to make. Place several teaspoonfulls of the dried or fresh herb in the bottom of the jar. Pour in the alcohol so that it just covers the herbs. Seal the jar and leave it alone for twenty-four hours. Then pour in more alcohol, about double the amount as before, and seal it again and leave it alone for one week. After one week, pour in double the amount of alcohol and seal and leave for two to four weeks. After this time the tincture is ready for use. Strain the liquid through a colander or cheesecloth and use a funnel to transfer it into storage in a smaller jar or eyedropper bottle. Tinctures will keep for up to six months if kept from heat and light.

Oil Blends

Oil blends are made by combining essential or aromatic oils and are the purest essence of the plant material. The best oil blends are those whose scents are given time to "marry," or to become the unique scent you seek, rather than being a mix of scent notes from all the ingredients.

To measure oils you will need a small collection of eyedroppers and eyedropper bottles in which to store your blends. These are available at low cost from most pharmacies. Start with a base oil that is non-irritating and of low scent, such as olive, safflower, or almond. Add your essential oils one drop at a time, keeping in mind the strength of the scents as you go. Remember that this is the strongest liquid form of any herb or plant. It takes very little of these volatile oils to produce a strong scent, and too much can irritate the skin. Keep records of your oil recipes so you can reproduce them later if you need to, and then store them away from light and heat. Turn the bottle several times a day to blend the oils. Within three to seven days the blend should be ready for use. Discard unused oil blends after twelve weeks.

Essential oils are volatile and usually toxic. Never ingest any product containing essential oils, and use them on your skin only in diluted form. Be aware of side effects such as allergies, rashes, and irritations, and photosynthetic reactions where the sun blemishes or stains the skin when it encounters an essential oil. The sun can also cause a blistering rash that looks and feels like poison ivy. Be cautious and know what it is you're using before you slather it on. The best magick is the magick that leaves you alive and healthy to enjoy the goal you brought into being.

Once you have made your products, you should dedicate them to your purpose by using the six spellcrafting procedures described earlier in this chapter. This brings in the last of your ingredients: you, the true source of all your successful magick.

two
The Magickal Bath

Tell them, dear, that if eyes were made for seeing,
Then beauty is its own excuse for being.
—Ralph Waldo Emerson

The magickal bath is a luxury that comes most often to mind when one thinks of bath and beauty spellcrafting. The very thought of this type of magick for most of us conjures up images of solitude, relaxation, daydreaming, and personal space teeming with magickal scents and sights. With the hectic schedule most of us keep, soaking in a warm tub is also a chance to have personal time to meditate and contemplate.

Bathing has always served more than just the hygienic function of bodily cleanliness. Baths have been drawn to soften the skin, enhance beauty, purify the spirit before religious ritual, relax, change internal body temperature, relieve sickness, and for making magick. The right ingredients in a magickal bath can enhance physical appearance and work magick with great effect.

Powdered herbs are recommended for bath use rather than dried, for purely practical reasons. Most common cooking herbs can be found already prepared as powdered. If you can't find them, then consider the magickal boost you'll get from powdering your own with an old-fashioned mortar and pestle. If you need to powder your own herbs and want to use a method less like churning your own butter, consider using a hand-powered kitchen chopper or a coffee grinder. Oils can also be used, with caution, and are easily worked into bath salt blends.

Most of the recipes in this chapter should not cause problems with your drain pipes, but please be aware that this possibility exists whenever you add anything to your bath water. On a daily basis just the dirt and hair from your body and residue from any soap can cause drainage problems, so imagine what herbs and other ingredients might do. If you are concerned about any spell clogging your pipes, it's best to tie up the ingredients in a cheesecloth or tea ball and place that in your bath instead. In fact, as someone who learned this lesson the hard way, just like all the lessons I seem to learn in magick, I recommend never using any nonwater-soluble substance in the tub without containing it first. This containment hurts nothing about either the spell or the beauty treatment. It simply becomes an infusion to impart the magickal energies of your spell into the bath without allowing the ingredients to be loose and taken down the drain when you're finished. Just remember to remove the container from the bath and bury the ingredients to ground them when you're finished.

Skin and Beauty Baths

The spells in this section are not just for appearance's sake. They are for drawing powerful magick into your life through the element of water and, sometimes, from fire in the form of accompanying candles. These are the two elements most often associated with magick that result in profound transformations of both the inner and outer selves.

The recipes found here are not a panacea for all skin and beauty woes. Magick helps those who help themselves. Soaking for hours in a beauty treatment for your skin is useless if you go out and expose it unprotected to the sun and wind every day. Commonsense care of the body should never be abandoned in favor of magick alone, but should be used in tandem for best results.

Healing Milk Bath

Milk is associated with healing energies and with enhancing psychic sensations. Considering its source and its nutrient richness it should come as no surprise that it is related to the moon and to the energy of the Mother Goddess. Milk is also reputed to help skin retain its youthful suppleness and acts as a mild astringent. Famous beauties French Queen Marie Antoinette (1755–1793) and Franco-American Broadway star Anna Held (1870–1918) were both reported to be avid fans of milk baths. Rich milks, including the powdered variety, are sometimes used to soothe minor skin irritations and rashes.

In a medium-sized glass mixing bowl, combine:

> 2½ cups powdered milk
>
> ¼ cup finely grated lime rind
>
> ⅛ teaspoon powdered allspice

This recipe should make enough for four to eight baths, depending on the size of the bathtub you use. The newer, more compact tubs—the ones that are blasted hard to get comfortable in—will require adding only about an eighth of the total recipe. The older, more commodious tubs will use closer to one quarter of the mixture per bath. Store the unused portion in a tightly sealed container. It will keep for about ten days if refrigerated.

Toss a small handful of the healing mixture into warm bath water. (Note: Cooler water may be in order if you're running a fever.) You may wish to light a blue or purple candle in the room if you can keep an eye on it and you are sure it will not be sitting where it could set fire to clothing or towels, or ignite some combustible substance on your countertop or vanity table. I like to place mine inside the sink where, even if it does tip over, it can't hurt anything.

You may also wish to burn some cedar or honeysuckle incense. Use caution if your bathroom is small. Incense is great for bringing into your spell both the element of air and the essence of the herb or flower used in the incense, but the fumes can be asphyxiating in a small space. Turn on your ventilator and use only as much incense as needed.

As you lower yourself into the tub, visualize the healing process beginning. Allow yourself to feel healing energy being pulled into your body from the ingredients of the mixture as you soak. While soaking you should repeat an affirmation, or a present-tense single sentence, stating your goal as if it was a fact right now. Examples are "I am healthy and whole" or "I have wonderful health and a strong immune system."

Keep in mind in all your magick that phrasing any words of power in the future tense will only keep your magick in the future, ever just out of your grasp. You don't want to always be dreaming of tomorrow. Visualize and verbalize your magick as if your goal exists today and it is much more likely to manifest today than in a tomorrow that never comes. Always, always phrase magickal wording in the present tense.

You may get out of the tub and continue with your daily routine whenever you're ready. However, if you are ill, do not forget to follow the orders of your doctor. Modern medicine derived much of its knowledge from herbal medicines and folk cures, and they work in perfect harmony when you have a doctor who is not blindly opposed to helping you select them. Magick for healing is but one weapon in your arsenal against sickness, not your cure-all.

Psychic Milk Bath

To turn the previous spell from a healing one to one whose goal is enhancing your psychic powers, use lemon rind instead of lime, and leave out the allspice. Add a silver coin or moonstone to the water, but be absolutely sure it will not be able to be sucked down the drain and that you will not be able to slip on it. If you like, you may add a little powdered marjoram to the mixture.

As you soak in the tub, visualizing your psychic energies being enhanced, chant words of power such as:

> *Lemon of sun and milk of moon,*
> *To all that is I now attune;*
> *Lemon of yellow and milk so white,*
> *What I see and feel is true and right.*

Milk Beauty Bath

Turn the Healing Milk Bath into a bath to enhance beauty by leaving out the lime rind and adding a tablespoon of vanilla extract and, if you like, some rose petals or dried rose hips. A cup of fresh rainwater is a nice addition if it's practical.

You might also consider including a single drop of Venusian green food coloring to help the spell connect you with the energies of the beauty Goddess, Venus. Green candles burning in the bathroom are also a benefit. Visualize the image of the face and body you wish to have as you soak.

Between the Worlds Bath

This magickal bath helps you to contact and work within the unseen worlds. It is used before divination, spirit contact, deity invocation, faery magick, conducting séances, astral projection, or guided meditations to help facilitate your journey between the worlds of humanity and spirit. It is also a formula that softens the skin and enhances personal appearance. This is a great image for those following Celtic spiritual paths since the land of spirit is also the home of the Tuatha De Danaan, the faery/divine race of old Ireland, who are said to be arrestingly lovely to look upon.

Do not try to make and store this recipe, as it doesn't keep well. Place the following ingredients in the bath within a cheesecloth or tea ball each time you wish to do this spell.

> 1 cup oatmeal (for earth and the moon)
>
> 2 tablespoons rice bran (for beauty and manifesting)

Oatmeal has a great reputation for softening the skin and soothing minor skin irritations, so using more than a single cup can't hurt you. Place the cheesecloth in a full bathtub then add:

> ½ cup honey (for fire and the sun)
>
> ½ cup apple cider vinegar (for otherworld energies)
>
> 1 tablespoon vanilla extract (for beauty)

Apple cider vinegar is a great softener for skin and hair. In Celtic mythology, apples guard the road to Avalon, the land of the deities and of the ancestor spirits.

Soak in the tub while visualizing the ease with which you are able to traverse the worlds. You may want to employ horse imagery since these noble beasts are archetypally associated with travel between realms of existence. As you soak, chant:

By the moon and by the sun,
All time and space in me are one;
I open my mind to worlds unseen,
Worlds of reality and worlds of dream.

I'm a mighty steed who knows no fear,
Hoofbeats echoing a mantra dear;
No barrier can stop me, nor being quell,
The travels I do so safe and so well.

Exit the tub while keeping your focus on your magickal goal and enact it as soon as is practical afterward for the best results. Having a big fluffy bathrobe to use as a magickal robe is a help here, as it makes for a quick transition from tub to magickal working space.

Energizing Bath for Passion or Courage

To evoke passion or courage you will need to combine the following ingredients in your tub. Again, this is not a mixture that keeps well, so resolve to make it fresh each time it is needed. This is also a mixture that you can give to someone else who needs a shot of lusty passion or a boost of bravery.

- ½ cup orange juice
- ⅛ cup lemon juice
- 1 drop cedar oil
- A pinch sage or 2 drops clary sage oil
- A pinch powdered nutmeg

If your goal is courage, play a drumming tape or recite a present-tense affirmation of your goal as you soak. If your goal is evoking passion, think sexy thoughts.

Relaxing and Purifying Bubble Bath

A bubble bath formula of any kind can be made by adding grated castile soap to the mixture. Castile soap is a gentle, olive-oil based soap from the Castile region of Spain that is often used in soap making for those who don't like using the borax and lye products popular in the complex soap-making rituals of North America. Castile soap is gratable, meltable, and hardens gently, which makes it perfect for magickal bath uses. Castile bubbles aren't as dramatic or long lasting as the chemical bubble inducers found in commercially prepared bubble bath products, but it's much gentler on your skin and a much better catalyst for your magick. Make sure you have pure castile soap that uses vegetable oils as a cleansing agent rather than lard or other animal fats.

This recipe makes enough for one bath.

½ cup grated castile soap

3 drops sandalwood oil

¼ teaspoon almond extract

⅛ teaspoon powdered hyssop

⅛ cup powdered kelp (optional)

When you're ready to exit the tub, be sure to drain it while you're still sitting in it. Visualize all the impurities and stress of your life draining away with the water. Get out of the tub only after it's empty.

Bath Salts

Bath salts used for spellcraft infuse the bath water with the energy of Mother Earth. Salts soften the water, enhance cleansing ability, help ground and protect the practitioner, and allow the proper diffusion of oils into the bath water so that they easily blend with the water and do not irritate the skin. Remember that oil and water do not mix and that many essential oils are irritants. Bath salt preparations help overcome both of these obstacles.

In beauty applications, salts are exfoliants and circulation stimulants for the skin. They increase the surface blood flow to give a rosy glow, slough off dead skin cells, and can soothe skin irritation or act as a softening agent. Sea salt has become a popular beauty treatment in recent years as a scrub rather than a bath treatment, but it can be harsh used in this way on all but the thickest skin and can cause tiny tears in the skin's surface. This is not attractive and can invite infection.

Salts can be stored in airtight containers for several years and rarely need refrigeration. I keep mine in those same glass jars that are sold in craft and hobby stores in December for storing gifts of candy and food. They have a tight plastic stopper around the inner rim that needs to be kept clean of salt and oils to avoid corroding, but so far I've had no problems. I label the jars with the name of the blend and sometimes add any astrological associations and information about the date and time the blend was made.

I used to keep bath salts in old margarine containers but abandoned that practice in short order. In a pinch they will work but they have no appeal to the magickal senses and they don't keep the salts fresh. More caution is required when using glass containers in the bath area, but so far I've not had any accidents. Just be aware of the possibility and be prepared to keep yourself, and all children or pets in your household, safe until the area is thoroughly cleaned of glass shards.

Some magickal practitioners like to color their bath salts to correspond to the magickal goal they seek. Vegetable-based food colorings, such as those discussed in the previous chapter, work well for this but have the same drawbacks of staining clothing, tubs, containers, and possibly your skin. If you want to use a color that you have to blend yourself from other food colorings, be sure to do the mixing before you add the coloring to the salts. If you don't premix, the salts will absorb the colors separately and thwart your efforts to blend them. The result will be a mottled look. Unless this is the effect you want to achieve, it will not make you happy with your resulting product, and this will reduce its magickal efficacy.

Magickal color association is very individualized. Though there are popular guidelines and some consensus among practitioners, you should not be afraid to use any color that feels right to you. When in extreme doubt about color choice it is always best to use white which, as luck would have it, is the color of the salt base and will require no changes on your part. The following color chart should offer some guidance to you if you've never before added color to your magick. Notice that many different magickal goals share more than one traditional color association.

Red. Courage, lust, passion, personal energy, stamina, God magick, mother Goddess magick, blood rituals, resurrection rituals, winter rituals, full moon rituals, sexual prowess, war, aggression, fire magick, sexual love, dancing, sacrificial deities.

Orange. Solar magick, God magick, friendship, attraction, attunement rituals, legal issues, autumn rituals, fire magick, personal crusades, many hobbies, sports, friendly competition.

Yellow. Communication, intellect, study, mental prowess, solar spells, God magick, spring rituals, attaining wisdom, air magick, summer rituals, fire magick, employment, money, travel, writing, games, story spells.

Green. Peace, relaxation, centering, harmony, Earth magick, eco-magick, fertility, money, beauty, prosperity, good luck, abundance, crop magick, love, spring and summer rituals, garden magick, faery magick, art, dancing.

Blue. Peace, sleep, dream magick, astral travel, tranquility, spirituality, virgin Goddess magick, singing, healing, psychicism, past-life explorations, fidelity, music, divination, music, song spells.

Violet. Hidden energy, rage, suppressed passions, communication with unseen beings, the higher self, connection to the divine, deep sleep, psychicism, healing, calm before the storm, banishing.

White. All magickal purposes especially spirituality, purification, exorcism, good luck, life and death, the virgin Goddess, lunar magick, new and full moon magick, egg magick, protection, attainment of the Godhead.

Black. Absorption, banishing, exorcism, the unknown, crone Goddess magick, autumn and winter rituals, stopping gossip, new moon magick, protection, reflective magick.

Silver. God or Goddess magick, lunar rituals, making wishes, psychicism, child-birth, pregnancy, astral travel, spirit contact, dream magick, the inner life, water magick, song.

Gold. God or Goddess magick, summer or autumn rituals, abundance, good luck, employment, money, solar rites, protection, crop magick, the work-place, the outer life.

Pink. Household peace, romantic love, puppy love, spring rituals, tranquility, harmony, balance.

Brown. Magick for animals, eco-magick, garden magick, faery magick, most hobbies and crafts, drumming, woodcrafting, dancing.

Note that in most cases colors can be combined to achieve the essence of two color energies in one. This doesn't always work. For instance, blending green and yellow to get the energy of both isn't a popular option. Most people find yellow-green a sickly color that does not contain the powerful energies of either yellow or green. By contrast, purple aptly contains the essence of both hot red and cool blue and is an example of a good color mixture. Remember that your mind does not work exactly like everyone else's and that you may need to experiment to find out what will and will not work for you.

You may also add to your bath salts the food extracts used for cooking, or you may use powdered herbs. Powdered herbs are a good substitute if you have very sensitive skin that cannot tolerate essential oils. Be aware that the scent will be much less powerful this way but the magick will not. You may also complicate the drain clogging problem with powdered herbs so use them sparingly. It only takes a little to give you the magickal energy you need.

Bath Salts Base

This is the recipe base that you will use to blend your oils to make your bath salts. This recipe will make three full cups of salts, enough for 18–20 baths, unless you have a really huge bathtub.

> 2 cups Epsom salts
>
> ½ cup baking soda
>
> ½ cup sea salt

Thoroughly mix the oils you are using in a separate container from the salt. Don't place them directly into the salt unless you are using only one oil. You want them to be absorbed evenly and produce a blended scent rather than little whiffs of different odors. Unless you are in a great hurry, it's best to allow your blended oils to sit for at least a few days to fully develop its own unique bouquet. This is called allowing the scents to "marry" or "bond." Gently turn the tightly capped bottle they are in several times a day and give them a boost of magickal empowerment. All this effort makes for a better-smelling blend and also allows you to put more time and energy into the oils that are the catalysts for your magickal desire.

If you wish to use color, add it after you've added the oils and herbs. These may be enough to give you a subtle color and you may find you're happy with it as is. If not, blend the food colorings together in a separate container before adding it to the salt. Mix it into the salts by hand, working the color through thoroughly and evenly.

Bath Oils

Bath oils can be used alone or they can be added to a bath salts mixture to help them blend with the water and counteract their skin-irritating properties. If you want to use an oil without salts you will need to place the oils in a neutral oil base first. This serves two purposes. First of all, it lessens the chances that the catalyst oils will irritate the skin and, second, it diffuses the potency of the essential oils. Essential oils are concentrated in the extreme. They are flammable, volatile, and sometimes harmful. Many essential oils are strong poisons even when the plants they are derived from are not.

Oils should be blended into a base oil with all the care and time given to the oil blends described in the bath salts recipe earlier in this chapter. Store oil blends in the dark glass eyedropper bottles you can purchase at pharmacies. The oils will stay fresh for several months if they are tightly capped and stored away from heat and light. Dispose of them sooner if they develop a rancid odor.

Oils should be blended by single drops and records should be kept of your mixtures. When you purchase your eyedropper bottles, be sure to get lots of extra eyedroppers. It's virtually impossible to clean the scent of other oil blends off them and you don't want to mix their energies. Also, the caustic properties of the oils will break down the rubber droppers and you will need to replace them frequently. For this reason, you should try to cap your stored oil blends with tops that do not have droppers attached. You'll go through less of them that way.

The amount of oil blend that you will need to add to your bath water is minute. This is because it is the energy of the oil rather than the oil itself that is helping you work your magick and because of the very real possibility of skin irritation. After you've soaked in the tub for awhile, your sense of smell will become immune to the scent and you may be tempted to add more oil. Don't. Some evaporation of essential oils occurs with heat, but not enough to do any damage to your spell. You only risk a very unmagickal itch if you overdo the oils.

After placing oils into a full tub of water, be sure to use a wooden spoon or other stirring utensil to break down all the oil beads that will collect on the water's surface. This is because your elementary school science teacher was right: Oil and water don't mix. Break down the droplets as much as possible to both disperse their energy and to avoid excessive contact with your skin.

Bath Oils Base

Fill a one-ounce eyedropper bottle two-thirds full of a base oil or mixture of base oils. One ounce is the standard size eyedropper, the one you are most likely to purchase at a pharmacy. If yours is smaller or larger, you will need to adjust the amount of oil you use accordingly since the blends in this chapter are calibrated for the two-thirds-of-one-ounce base. Choose from any one or all of the following base oils. I have listed them in my order of preference, but you should choose the one(s) that work best for you.

Olive
Almond
Safflower
Canola
Apricot Kernel
Coconut

Magickal Bath Salt and Bath Oil Blends

Don't feel you have to slavishly follow these or any other spells. Spells are mutable. They are not set in stone. They are maps that show but one route to a final destination. One spell may work fast and well for a friend and fail for you simply because you resonate differently with one of the ingredients. No one said magick would be easy or that it didn't take some trial and error.

If you find you have only one of the ingredients listed, then use it. Don't feel you have to embark on a quest for a specific oil. Single-oil blends have a noble history. The single-oil method is actually best for magickal beginners, who can only focus on one idea or catalyst for any length of time. Single-scent oil blends don't cloud the desired outcome with extra energies.

You may substitute any ingredients as long as they are not poisonous and you know they will not cause an allergic reaction. This idea of substituting ingredients causes great trepidation among magickal newcomers. It's good to be cautious and thoughtful about your magick, but don't let it ruin the joy of magick for you. When in doubt about an ingredient, the best thing to do is to have a magickal herbal guide on hand to help you select. The references section in the back of this book lists several that are invaluable, even for the long-time practitioner of the magickal arts. Buying one is not a big expense but it will be one of the best investments of your magickal life. My favorite is dog-eared and stained from years of use, and I never loan it to anyone.

Measure your essential oils drop by single drop into either the base oil if making an oil blend, or into a separate glass container that has a tight cap if you will be using the oils to make bath salts. Make a record of any changes or experiments you do and, in a Book of Shadows or magickal diary, record the time, place, and date you made the blend and leave room to record the results later on. This will help you track what works best for you so, if needed, you can do it again.

For Assisting in Astral Projection

3 drops mugwort

2 drops benzoin

1 drop camphor

Astral projection will be discussed in more depth in a later chapter. If you are unsure of the process for out-of-body travel, use this oil before going to bed to assist you in stepping out of your dreams and into the astral realm.

To Give Comfort and Consolation

3 drops lemon balm

2 drops yarrow

1 drop marigold

1 drop geranium

This makes an excellent gift for someone who is grieving. Package it in a pretty jar and offer it with an appropriate sympathy card.

Finding Romance

6 drops jasmine

4 drops lavender

2 drops vanilla

2 drops orange blossom

Purification

7 drops sandalwood

2 drops lotus or 1 drop ylang ylang

1 drop black pepper

The act of bathing is always purifying, but in-depth spiritual and emotion purification are often needed before many magickal rituals, and this blend can help.

Inducing Lust

2 drops allspice

1 drop clove

1 drop neroli or bergamot (*Mentha citrata*)

1 drop basil

This is a great bath blend to use when you have a tub big enough for two.

Halting Gossip

8 drops orange

2 drops nutmeg

1 drop clove

Make sure to visualize the negative energy of gossip draining away from you as the tub drains.

Enhancing Beauty #1

6 drops rose

3 drops jasmine

3 drops lotus

Enhancing Beauty #2

3 drops lavender

2 drops vanilla

2 drops apple blossom

Protection

3 drops basil

2 drops allspice

1 drop black pepper

This blend works for both psychic and physical protection, and works best in tandem with commonsense protection efforts.

Fertility

4 drops myrrh

2 drops cypress

2 drops lemon

This blend works best when both partners use it, either separately or in the same bath.

Courage

6 drops lime

3 drops carnation

½ drop thyme (extreme skin irritant)

Mental Prowess

7 drops rosemary

1 drop peppermint or 2 drops wintergreen

Use this blend before studying or the night before a big exam. Add a drop or two of lilac oil to help improve your memory.

Psychic Enhancement

5 drops jasmine

5 drops coconut (cold pressed, not essential)

5 drops magnolia

Engage in your psychic endeavor as soon as possible after bathing for best results.

Exorcism or Banishment

3 drops frankincense

1 drop clove or bay

Finding Friendship

4 drops peppermint

4 drops lemon verbena

Balance and Harmony

    4 drops sandalwood

    3 drops myrrh

    2 drops chamomile

    1 drop vervain

Balance and harmony can refer to inner beauty as well. You might use this formula with words of power adapted from Plato, the famous third century B.C.E. Greek philosopher and teacher, who said:

> *Grant that I may become beautiful in my soul within,*
> *and that all my external possessions be in harmony*
> *with my inner self.*

Making Spirit Contact

    3 drops lavender

    3 drops vetivert

    ½ drop cinnamon (strong skin irritant)

Tranquility and Sleep

    9 drops apricot (cold pressed, not essential)

    4 drops lemon verbena

    2 drops acacia (*Acacia senegal*)

    1 drop rosewood

    1 drop bergamot

For best results, plan to go to a place where you can be alone to relax, or plan to go to bed as soon as possible after using this blend.

For Lunar Rituals

    8 drops ylang ylang

    4 drops myrrh

    2 drops magnolia

    1 drop lemon

Healing

6 drops carnation

3 drops rosemary

1 drop coriander

1 drop spearmint

Overcoming Obstacles

3 drops coriander

1 drop cardamom (*Elettario cardamomum*)

1 drop clove

Use these formulas while reading and imagining visions of powerful women. Mythology is a good source for finding these. One of my personal favorites is Queen Maeve of Connacht from Irish mythology, a warrior who had an insatiable lust for life and who let nothing stand in the way of obtaining what she wanted.

Gaining Money

2 drops nutmeg

2 drops copal

2 drops ginger

1 drop patchouly

Finding Employment

6 drops orange

3 drops pine

1 drop cedarwood

1 drop juniper

three
Soap and Shower Magick

She walks in beauty like the night
Of cloudless climes and starry skies;
And all that's best of dark and bright
Meet in her aspect and her eyes.
—George Gordon (Lord Byron)

Few daily tasks make us feel as fresh, renewed, and healed as a shower. Shower magick is among the easiest of magicks to make and has the added benefit of being both relaxing and invigorating. Almost all dwellings constructed from the 1960s onward have showers. Sometimes newer homes and apartments don't have bathtubs but they will have shower stalls with options like massage settings or therapeutic jet sprays.

As opposed to the bathtub, the shower is constantly draining itself as you use it, making it a natural for visualizing yourself being rid of something unwanted. For help in focusing that visualization, simply gaze at the water spinning down the drain as you work your shower magick.

I have always been an advocate of the bathroom as a space for magick and meditation. It's one of the few rooms in a home that's designed for total privacy. Most have doors that lock and send a strong "do not disturb" message to other members of your household. In many modern homes and apartments the bathroom comes without a window to the outside world, which adds to the aura of solitude and helps cut down on distracting noises. If there does happen to be a window, it's often adorned with frosted glass or overlooks the more private areas of your property. All these factors help keep the bathroom dark so that spells requiring darkness work very well, even during daylight hours.

The bathroom also has lots of fireproof surfaces for candles and censors such as porcelain, tile, and stainless steel. This is wonderful for candle magick because it lessens the danger of an accident burning the place down. Yet the bathroom is less of a boon to the burning of incense as it is to candles. Incense can be overpowering in a small room without adequate ventilation, and even dangerous if you're using charcoals with chemical ignition products in them. Scents are magnified tenfold in the warm dampness of the bathroom and should be used sparingly.

Homemade shower products are easy and fun to make. They cleanse and beautify as they work as catalysts for your magickal goals. The recipes given here for soaps and soaks can be altered to suit virtually any magickal need. As you go through them, selecting the ones that best fit your desires, and find that you really like part of one and part of another, don't be afraid to combine them. Just keep in mind any interactions or side effects they might cause and any allergies you might have. See Appendix B for a list of precautions and possible interactions of herbs and oils. Otherwise there is no need to be slavish to these recipes any more than you would be to any other spell not created by yourself for yourself.

The following is a list of specific actions, both magickal and physical, that are garnered from various ingredients. This chart will be referred to throughout the next several chapters as we pull together items that will best enhance your hair, skin, and spells.

This list of magickal actions is far from complete. Consult books on magickal herbalism for more information. The names of several good books on the subject can be found in the References section in the back of this book.

Desired Soap Action and Active Ingredients

Astringent. Rosemary, witch hazel, cream of tartar, egg whites, hazelnut oil, grapeseed oil.

Exfoliates. Lemon juice, apple juice, vinegar, milk, salts, caraway seed, poppy seed, barley, brown sugar.

Heals and Plumps. Vitamin E oil, aloe vera, amaranth.

Heals Chapping. Beeswax, camphor oil, petroleum jelly, cardamom oil, lard.

Heat Producing. Ginger, cayenne, cinnamon.

Moisturizes. Avocado, pumpkin, neroli oil, cocoa butter, glycerin, lanolin, wheat germ oil, oatmeal, rose decoction, banana, apricot kernel oil, banana.

Soap Agents. Castile soaps, borax, cream of tartar, wood ash, salts, potassium hydroxide, palm oil, rosin, sulfonated castor oil, lye.

Softens Skin. Almond oil, coconut oil, glycerin, lanolin, oatmeal, castor oil, mineral oil, honey, wheat germ oil.

Soothes. Aloe vera, wheat germ, cornmeal, apple cider vinegar, birch, rice bran, honey, psyllium, gelatin, cucumber, rose.

Sunscreen. Birch bark powder, sesame seed oil.

Takes Out Redness. Cornstarch, potato, black alder, tea tree oil, white sugar.

Desired Magickal Action and Catalysts

Astral Projection. Mugwort, parsley, eyebright, amaranth, basil, chicory, mistletoe, tumbleweed, poplar.

Beauty. Melissa, violet, briony, ginseng, maidenhair, cardamom, geranium, ylang ylang, peach, rose, neroli, tuberose, ginger (weight loss), yerba santa, vanilla, lovage, oats, jojoba, clary sage (*Salvia sclarea*), hazelnut, chamomile.

Binding. Willow, knotweed (*Polygonum aviculare*), ivy.

Brain Power. Rosemary, sage, caraway seed, cowslip, ginger, goldenseal, marjoram, woodruff, sesame seed, horehound, eyebright, spearmint, carrot.

Comfort. Lemon balm, marigold, skullcap, dulse (*Rhodymenia palmata*).

Communication. Cumin, rosemary, dandelion, European broom, parsley, sage, aspen.

Courage. Sweet pea, columbine, thyme, yarrow, grapefruit, balsam oil.

Creativity. Clover, blackberry, rosemary, cowslip.

Curse Breaking. Copal, galangal, vetivert, toadflax (*Linaria vulgaris*), thistle, lime, dragon's blood, jojoba.

Dream Magick. Mugwort, jasmine, bracken, mimosa, catnip, chamomile, cedarwood, acacia.

Exorcism. Frankincense, black pepper, fumitory, tamarind, sagebrush, snapdragon, dragon's blood, larkspur, balsam oil, yarrow.

Faery Magick. Hawthorn, cowslip, primrose, lilac.

Fertility. Bistort, carrot juice, almond oil, nuts, rice, wheat, hazel, patchouly, banana, pomegranate, fig, dock, acorn, poppy, corn oil, cornmeal, hazelnut.

Fidelity. Chickweed, ivy, elder, anise, yerba maté, cumin, nutmeg, rue, corn, sweet clover oil.

Friendship. Yerba maté (*Ilex paraguaiensis*), meadowsweet, passionflower, sweet pea, lemongrass, pineapple.

Gossip, Halts. Clove, orris root, knotweed, houndstongue.

Grounding. Salts, ashes, patchouly, clay, stones.

Helps Heal. Aloe vera, willow, goldenseal, allspice, mint, pine, thyme, oak, sandalwood, carnation, rosemary, camphor, fennel, hyssop, eucalyptus, elder, wintergreen, rosemary, mint, raspberry, acacia.

Love and Romance. Apple blossom, orange blossom, jasmine, lavender, rose, vanilla, rosemary, apricot, palmarosa, tuberose, mullein, vervain, yarrow, rue, myrtle, hyacinth, peach, sandalwood, lemon verbena, basil, coltsfoot, columbine, marjoram, violet, tamarind, meadowsweet, barley, gentian, catnip, clary sage, strawberry, kyphi (*Kyphi tsa Egyptian*), sweet clover oil, acacia.

Lust, Increases. Hibiscus, cinnamon, peppermint, rosemary, clove, ginger, dill, fenugreek, basil, carrot, ginseng, black cohosh, deerstongue, damiana, cypress.

Lust, Decreases. Camphor, skullcap, clary sage.

Money and Job. Orange, nutmeg, patchouly, cypress, vetivert, comfrey, goldenrod, wheat, moss, vervain, goldenseal, woodruff, vetivert, cinquefoil, clove, cinnamon, cedar, ginger, alfalfa, allspice, bergamot, jojoba, grapefruit, honesty (*Lunaria* spp.).

Obstacles. Sweet pea, thistle, ginger, rowan, black cohosh, columbine, thyme, yarrow, moonwort, mistletoe, chicory.

Past-Life Viewing. Lilac oil, amaranth, mimosa.

Peace and Calm. Lavender, violet, gardenia, lavender, linden blossom, chamomile, catnip, agrimony, vervain, lemon balm, marigold, sugar, dulse, loosestrife, catnip.

Protection. Cinnamon, thyme, bay, clove, black pepper, agrimony, betony, burdock, blackberry, orris root, yucca root, cactus, mimosa, eucalyptus, frankincense, cedar, cumin, papaya, honeysuckle, myrrh, cypress, birch, ashes, moss, briony, clay, dill, elder, fenugreek, buckthorn, rowan, Spanish moss, mulberry, cardamom, arbutus, balsam, citronella.

Psychic Power. Wormwood, catnip, valerian, orris root, mimosa, eyebright, yarrow, acacia, borage, honeysuckle, peppermint, bistort, flax seed, mastic, elecampane, angelica.

Purification. Sandalwood, frankincense, copal, lavender, turmeric, hyssop, cedar, lavender, yucca root, vervain, fennel, myrrh, valerian, angelica, lemon, benzoin.

Rituals, Lunar. Lotus, jasmine, myrrh, ylang ylang, chickweed, coconut oil, sandalwood, gardenia, cucumber, lemon, wintergreen, eucalyptus, lily.

Rituals, Solar. Acacia, orange, nutmeg, copal, rosemary, chicory, sesame, sunflower oil or seed, St. John's Wort, ginseng, benzoin, angelica.

Spirit Contact. Cinnamon, wormwood, ylang ylang, lavender, sweetgrass, mastic, thistle, dandelion, apple, sage, linden, amaranth.

Spirituality. Sandalwood, copal, gotu kola, myrrh, oak moss.

Weather Magick. Holly (lightning), borage (wind), bracken (rain), hemp (wind), heather (rain).

Solid Soaps

No one would argue that solid soaps are more complicated to make than gel soaps, but they also offer us more creative challenges. Please don't be tempted to skip this section because of your preconceived ideas about the onerous soap-making process. Get that image of some hillbilly granny stirring a bubbling cauldron of lung-searing lye out of your head, and slide your mind into the twenty-first century, where everything is much easier to do than it was in times past. The solid soap recipes appearing in this book are not made of lye or borax, will not leather your skin or corrode your lungs, and they will not require a grocery store full of exotic ingredients or an entire day to make. (If you are interested in the complete and complex art of old-fashioned soap making, I found Susan Miller Cavitch's *The Natural Soap Book* [Storey Books, 1995] to be both thorough and readable.)

Lye and other caustic agents have been used in making soaps not out of ignorance, but because some type of caustic agent is necessary to make soap clean. Tallow and coconut have been used as substitutes and, while they are gentler to the skin, they don't clean as well. If you want to add lye or borax as a caustic agent, these ingredients are available through soap-making suppliers. See Appendix A for resources.

I love creating solid soaps for magickal purposes. Because of the hardness of solid soap and the fact that you use only a small layer of it at a time, you have so many more choices than with bath and beauty items into which you can place almost nothing except essential oils. In solid soaps you can use salts, meals, extracts, and dried herbs too.

A precaution to be offered with this wide range of ingredient possibilities is the need to protect your drain pipes. I recommend going to a hardware store and buying one of those small wire colanders that fit over your drain and trap anything larger than a pebble. Take the protection one step further and cover this with cheesecloth when you will be showering with magickal items that could clog your pipes. This will make the draining process more sluggish, but it saves you headaches in the end.

All the solid soap recipes should be melted with grated, solid castile soap. How much castile soap you use will depend on how many soap molds you want to fill. The recipes in this chapter are designed for making two bars about the size of seven-ounce tuna fish cans. Be sure to line cans of any nonstore-bought molds with wax paper to make them easy to remove once hardened.

You can use tuna cans, soup cans, small cartons, etc., or you can buy soap and candy molds from specialty stores or craft shops. Molds come in a variety of sizes and shapes, many that suit magickal needs or have seasonal themes. I've seen molds in the shape of stars (for power), roses (for love and beauty), trees (for strength), eggs (for fertility), rabbits (for spring rites), moons (for psychicism), sunbursts (for summer and winter rites), and almost any other imaginable figure. You may want to just browse what's available and see if anything inspires you.

You don't need a lot of equipment for these simple, solid soaps. You will need a glass pan or glass double boiler for melting the grated castile soap and blending the ingredients. Don't use metal or you could harm your nonstick finish. Dried soap is harder to remove than burned cheese and will take some serious scraping to remove, even from glass. Disposable wooden spoons are also good to have on hand.

Place all the soap ingredients in the glass pan or in the top of the double boiler and turn the heat to a medium-low temperature. Don't try to rush the melting process with higher temperatures. High heat will alter the scent of the blend and could cause volatile oils to burst into flame.

Stir constantly, moving your spoon clockwise for spells whose goal is the increase of something and counterclockwise for spells whose goal is to decrease something. Don't forget to visualize and to use any chosen words of power throughout every step of your soap's creation. When the ingredients seem well blended, you can remove the pan from the heat.

Allow the soap to sit untouched for about ten minutes, then pour or spoon the liquid into the mold. Allow it to cool for about an hour. Place the molds in the freezer overnight so they will harden all the way through.

It's a good idea to have smaller soap molds on hand to use up leftover melted soap. For instance, have a tray of small candy molds at hand for making the leftovers. They make wonderful travel soaps so you can take your magick with you when you need to be away from home. They also give you something "risk free" to do with the unused portion still in the melting pan.

Never pour the unused portion of the soap down a drain. If you've ever had or heard of a grease clog from cooking residue that blocks pipes, they are nothing compared to the viciousness of melted soap when it hardens. Pour the leftover soap into an empty food can or plastic garbage bag if you must, but don't be tempted to take the easy route down your drain pipes.

When you remove the soap from the freezer, you should allow about an hour before trying to remove it from the mold. This allows it to come out more easily and cuts down on breakage.

Wrap the completed soaps in wax paper or place them in the covered soap containers travelers use. Don't try to place them in airtight containers, as they will sweat and break down faster. Hardened soaps will keep for several months, longer if refrigerated. They will keep for a year or two if preservatives are added. The Resources appendix in the back of this book has the names of some vendors who sell soap-making supplies that include preservatives if this is what you want. Without preservatives, the oils and other natural ingredients will not keep as long in the warm dampness of your bathroom.

There are optional items you can add to any of the soap recipes in this chapter. You may add a little food coloring to the soap mixture, based on your magickal goal. Look to the chart in the previous chapter for ideas. However, you may find that the natural color of the castile soap mixed with the herbs will produce a color you like. Use color sparingly to avoid staining skin, tubs, and towels.

You may also add oatmeal or salt to any soap. Oatmeal softens and soothes, and salt exfoliates. If you are undergoing professional dermatological processes, such as dermabrasion or laser peels, don't use any aromatic oil or salt on your skin. Your skin will be much too sensitive and you could do lasting damage. Likewise, if you are being treated for any skin disease, rash, or if you have acne, consult your doctor before using any noncommercial beauty product.

I'm fond of placing a surprise item inside homemade soaps corresponding to their magickal goals. For example, I'll add a lodestone or magnet to a soap designed for attraction, a silver coin for a soap that seeks to aid in the seeking of prosperity, an acorn in a soap whose goal is fertility, or a peach pit in a soap created to bring inner peace. As these items appear to manifest from the lather and work their way from the soap as it is used, this visual image helps to reinforce the idea that the magick is manifesting, coming into being in the physical world.

If you wish to add a surprise in the center of your soap you will need to make its creation a two-day process. Use only half the soap recipe and fill the mold only halfway full. Cool and freeze it. The next day place the surprise in the center of the mold. Make the other half of the recipe, finish filling the mold, then cool and freeze the soap.

Some recipes call for purées, which are simply forms of a food substance that have been blended to be more liquid, but not runny. For instance, applesauce is a form of purée. Most kitchen blenders have a purée setting that can be used to transform foods from solids to purées. The more purée you add to any beauty product, the more you cut its shelf life, simply because nonrefrigerated food substances only last about a week. Keep this in mind when adding food purées to any soap.

Beauty Soap #1

¼ cup oatmeal

1 tablespoon honey

1 teaspoon almond oil

¾ cup grated castile soap

By oatmeal and honey, by this soap,
Viewed as a beauty by all in my scope,
Blessed is my being with an attractive glow,
I'm seen as desirable by all I know.

This is a soap blend best for dry skin. Adding Venusian green food coloring is optional. The oatmeal is a skin softener and the almond oil moisturizes. Remember when adding oatmeal that it will swell when wet, so don't be tempted to add lots more to a recipe because it doesn't look like enough when it's dry.

Beauty Soap #2

¼   cornmeal or powdered milk

1   tablespoon cornstarch

1   teaspoon baking soda

1   teaspoon witch hazel

1   teaspoon tea tree oil

½   cup grated castile soap

This is a soap blend that's best for oily skin. It contains tea tree oil, which has a reputation of helping combat acne without the dryness associated with commercial acne products. Add to this visualization by "seeing" the oils—and anything else about yourself you find less than attractive—being pulled down the drain away from you.

Beauty Soap #3

¼   cup dried maidenhair fern

2   tablespoons mashed potatoes

2   tablespoons honey

1   teaspoon vanilla extract

¼   teaspoon crushed caraway seeds

3   drops cardamom oil

1   cup grated castile soap

Adding a peach pit to the center of beauty soap can help reinforce the visualization of your beauty emerging as the soap is used.

Love Attracting Soap #1

¼ cup dried orange blossoms

1 tablespoon dried yarrow

½ teaspoon orris root powder

6 drops apple blossom oil

1 teaspoon vanilla extract

1¼ cups grated castile soap

By this lather that on me I slather,
I draw to me love from below and above;
From far and near I'm loved so dear,
I draw love to me, and so mote it be.

Love attracting soaps are nice to make in heart-shaped soap molds. If you want to add food coloring, try red or pink.

Love Attracting Soap #2

2 tablespoons dried mullein

2 tablespoons dried vervain

2 tablespoons brown sugar

4 drops columbine or jasmine oil

1 teaspoon apricot kernel oil

2 tablespoons grated beeswax

1½ cups grated castile soap

As you use this soap, burning jasmine or lavender incense in the bathroom with you—providing you have enough space and ventilation—can add to this spell.

Love Attracting Soap #3

¼ cup peach pulp

1 tablespoon dried lemon verbena

1 tablespoon dried meadowsweet

3 drops angelica oil

1 cup grated castile soap

Love Attracting Soap #4

¼ cup oatmeal

3 tablespoons grated orange rind

2 tablespoons grated lime rind

2 tablespoons cornstarch

½ teaspoon vanilla extract

¼ teaspoon tea tree oil

2 drops cedar oil

2 drops nutmeg oil

¾ cup grated castile soap

This soap has the citrusy, woodsy odor we associate with men's colognes. It makes a good gift for a man you know who is hoping to attract love into his life. The oatmeal will help soften his skin and the tea tree oil will provide a pleasant tingle.

Fidelity Forever Soap

¼ cup dried rue

2 tablespoons crushed anise seed

⅛ teaspoon dried cumin

1¾ cups grated castile soap

I give the gift of love that's true,
I give this fidelity magick to you;
Each time you wash from head to toe,
Your ties to me much stronger grow.

Your eyes to others never stray,
Your trust I'm sure of night and day;
To me you give soul, heart, and mind,
In faith everlasting I you bind.

You can use this soap yourself if you need to give your commitment to a person, goal, or promise a boost. You can also use it in the shower with your domestic partner or lover, or you can give it as a gift to someone you want remaining faithful to you. Wrap the gift soap in blue tissue paper and tie it with twine to seal the spell. Blue food coloring is optional in this soap.

The words of power given for this spell correspond to the gift-giving scenario. Be aware that as a gift this soap becomes a type of binding spell which, if the recipient is unaware of the nature of the gift, constitutes negative magick.

Fertility Soap

¼ cup pomegranate purée

¼ cornmeal

1 tablespoon almond oil

2 drops patchouly oil (optional to add scent)

3 tablespoons carnuba wax

1 cups grated castile soap

Both men and women may use this soap before making love when your goal is to become pregnant. It is a nice magickal boost, but not a necessity, if the moon is full during your fertile time of the month. Add moon energy to the soap with a drop or two of myrrh oil.

Healing Soap #1

¼ cup dried hyssop

⅛ cup dried rosemary

2 tablespoons cornstarch

6 drops sandalwood oil

3 drops carnation oil

¾ cup grated castile soap

continued . . .

By Airmid's wisdom and Diancecht's spell,
I bathe to make me whole and well;
By the caduceus wand and the unicorn's horn,
Good health and wellness in me is reborn.

This healing spell calls on Irish healing deities Airmid and her father Diancecht. The caduceus wand, a staff with two snakes entwining their way up the staff, is the symbol of modern medicine, and the unicorn horn is a fabled cure-all.

Add to the power of this spell by visualizing anything that is making you ill being pulled from you by the healing soap and being pulled down the drain away from you.

Healing Soap #2

¼ cup oatmeal

¼ apple purée or unsweetened applesauce

¼ teaspoon baking soda

1 cup grated castile soap

Add one or two drops of an essential oil to this for scent. Ones that work well in healing spells are pine, sandalwood, carnation, rosemary, wintergreen, camphor, or allspice. Thyme is another good healing oil but is a strong skin irritant.

While using this, any corresponding incense is nice to add to your bathroom, providing you have the room and good ventilation. If you prefer to burn candles or use food coloring, try purple, indigo, or blue.

Chakra Balancing Soap

1 drop patchouly oil for the root chakra

⅛ teaspoon crushed borage for the navel chakra

⅛ teaspoon powdered nutmeg for the solar plexus chakra

1 teaspoon vanilla extract for the heart center chakra

⅛ teaspoon ground cumin for the throat chakra

2 tablespoons dried mugwort for the third eye chakra

½ teaspoon dried acacia for the crown chakra

1¾ cups grated castile soap

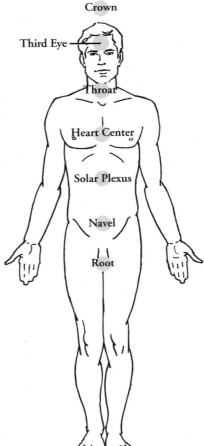

Crown

Third Eye

Throat

Heart Center

Solar Plexus

Navel

Root

Root of red for grounding,
Navel of orange for will;
Solar Plexus of yellow for feeling,
A green Heart as clear as a bell.
The Throat of blue speaks clearly,
The Third Eye of indigo can see;
The Crown of violet tops me,
My chakras, balanced be.

The chakras are the energy centers that run up and down the vertical center of the human body. They must remain somewhat open to allow the proper flow of energies to and from yourself and others and between all the operating systems of your body, mind, and spirit. This soap will stimulate, open, cleanse, and balance the chakra centers from root to crown. (The study of the chakras is a subject unto itself. I recommend Anodea Judith's *Wheels of Life* [Llewellyn, 1982] for beginners.)

Prosperity Soap

¼ cup crushed alfalfa

¼ pumpkin pulp or canned purée

2 tablespoons cornstarch

⅛ teaspoon ground allspice

6 drops bergamot oil (optional)

2 tablespoons grated beeswax

1 cup grated castile soap

If you want to add something to the center of this one, try a single gold coin or add a tablespoon of gold glitter from your local craft store. This soap is also a great skin softener with the pumpkin added.

Passion Soap #1

2 tablespoons carrot purée

1 tablespoon dried hibiscus

⅛ teaspoon powdered ginger

2 drops liquid dragon's blood

By my will your passion I claim,
The wild heart in me to tame;
Flame of lusty interest I light,
Your passion for me I do ignite.

Passion Soap #2

2 tablespoons crushed dill

1 teaspoon dried basil

1 teaspoon ginseng

⅛ teaspoon powdered fenugreek

2 drops peppermint oil

1¾ cups grated castile soap

We shall lust, and you must trust,
My passion's true as my love for you.

Passion Killing Soap

¼ cup pumpkin pulp or canned purée

3 tablespoon crushed pumpkin seeds

1 tablespoon powdered or dried skullcap

3 drops camphor oil

2 drops allspice oil (optional for scent)

Quenched must be our passion's flame,
I release you now and cast no blame;
What we shared was strong and deep,
But it was not a passion to keep.
Loves may come and loves may go,
Plant love elsewhere and reap what you sow.
I wish you well as we learn to go on,
And may our next loves not be wrong.

There are times when you just want the attachments of passion and love to go away. It may be because the relationship has run its course, or perhaps because you realize this person is not good for you or is unattainable. In any case, sometimes we all need a little help to get over someone with whom we've been in a passionate romance.

Add to the visualization of this spell by visualizing all the attachment you have for this person being pulled down the drain and away from you forever.

Adding a little scent you like to this soap can make a great gift to give to someone who needs some help in this area. You can also give it to someone you want to get over their feelings of attachment for you.

When I was doing research for *Bewitchments* (Llewellyn, 2000), my book on love magick, I was looking into the use of pumpkin seeds as a catalyst to banish an unwanted lover from your life and discovered an interesting side note. Medicinally, pumpkin seeds act as an anthelmintic, or a substance that rids the body of worms and parasites. If you think about it, the correlation is very amusing, and humor is one of the greatest boosters available for any magickal operation.

Purification Soap

¼ cup wheat germ

1 teaspoon dried and crushed copal

3 drops frankincense or benzoin oil

1 cup grated castile soap

The wheat germ in this soap also acts as a mild exfoliant and moisturizer.

Add to the visualization of this spell by "seeing" impurities that hold you back from your goals being sucked down the shower drain.

Fire Soap

2 tablespoons dried galangal

2 tablespoons dried rosemary

2 tablespoons dried amaranth or sweet pea

2 tablespoons dried fennel

2 tablespoons grated beeswax

1½ cups grated castile soap

You may add one to three drops of scent as you desire. Spicy fragrances most often correspond magickally to the fire element.

Use this soap when preparing to work magick associated with the element of fire. This can be something as obvious as candle magick or scrying (gazing for prophetic visions) in a fireplace, or it can be a spell associated with the element of fire. Fire-governed spells include those whose goal is transformation, lust, passion, sex, courage, stamina, strength, employment, banishment, and exorcism. Food colorings to try are red, orange, yellow, or gold.

You can also add these fire elements to any other magickal soap you feel could have its efficacy boosted by calling upon the energies of fire.

Flames of my will, rise ever higher,
As I call upon the powers of fire.

Air Soap

⅓ cup dried lemon verbena

⅓ cup dried parsley

1 teaspoon baking soda

1½ cups grated castile soap

You may add one to three drops of oil to scent the soap as you like. Mint, anise, and bergamot are good air-related oils to try if you aren't sure which ones to use. Suggested food colorings are blue and yellow.

Use this soap when preparing to work magick associated with the element of air. This can be wind magick or a spell whose goal is connected with communication, speech, writing, astral projection, meditation, study, school, travel, or thought over distance. You can also add these air elements to any other magickal soap you feel could have its efficacy boosted by calling on air's energies.

O sylphs of the east, so light and fair,
Bless my spell with the power of air.

Earth Soap

¼ cup buckwheat

¼ cup rice bran

2 tablespoons cornstarch

1 cup grated castile soap

You have the option of adding one to three drops of scent if you'd like. Earth scents to try include magnolia, primrose, tulip, cypress, and honeysuckle. Patchouly is probably the classic earth scent, but its heady smell can be overpowering, so use it sparingly. Suggested colorings for this soap are green and brown.

Use this soap when preparing to work magick associated with the earth element. Earth-governed spells include those whose goal is grounding, centering, balancing, friendship, prosperity, fertility, stability, and spells concerning the home or animals.

You can also add earth elements to any other magickal soap you feel could have its efficacy boosted by calling on the earth's energies.

By my home and by my hearth,
I garner the powers of Mother Earth.

Water Soap

¼ cup strawberry purée

¼ cup dried vervain

1 cup grated castile soap

Optional scents for water soap might be jasmine, lemon, gardenia, sandalwood, lotus, or lilac. Add one to three drops if you desire to scent your soap.

Use this soap as a preparation for magick associated with the element of water. This can be something as obvious as water scrying, bath magick, or purification rites. Water-governed areas of magick include childbirth, psychicism, divination, dream magick, beauty, love, romance, dancing, spirituality, and moon magick. Suggested colorings for this soap are blue, violet, lavender, or silver.

You can also add water elements to any other magickal soap you feel could have its efficacy boosted by calling uon the energies of water.

The power of water through me now flows,
My will makes magick wherever it goes.

Faery Soap

3 tablespoons grated beeswax

3 tablespoons powdered milk

2 tablespoons dried sweetgrass or hawthorn

2 tablespoons dried primrose or cowslip

2 tablespoons safflower oil

5 drops lilac or primrose oil

Use this soap when you want to align yourself with the energies of the faery realm or to contact the faery folk.

Good Hostess Soap

¼ cup crushed pineapple

1 tablespoon dried loosestrife

1 tablespoon dried lemon balm

1 tablespoon honey

3 drops gardenia oil

1 cup grated castile soap

Blessed Lord Bacchus, grant me your most,
Calm my jitters so I can be a good host;
May earthly pleasures for all here be found,
May this gathering be joyful and good cheer abound.

No one who has ever stood in the shower an hour before party guests are due to arrive has not been nervous about their abilities to make everyone comfortable and content for an evening. This soap will help soothe your nerves and pave the way for a fun event for everyone. The words of power call on Bacchus, Roman God of revelry and hedonism, to offer his blessing to your gathering. It also helps to burn orange candles for camaraderie and friendship at your party. If they are scented with bergamot or neroli, even better.

Distance Lends Enchantment Soap

¼ cup grated beeswax

2 tablespoons dried cumin

1 teaspoon dried aspen or bladderwrack

4 drops amaranth oil

1 cup grated castile soap

As you use this soap, turn yourself in the four cardinal directions and ask those elements to assist you in carrying your message to your distant lover. The evocation might sound something like the following:

Powers of fire, burn me into
the mind of (lover's name) with
thoughts of passion and longing.
Powers of water, wash over (lover's name)
and drown him in feelings of love.
Powers of earth, let (lover's name)
know I am the stable ground he
walks upon, his foundation.

continued . . .

Powers of air, carry my love and
thoughts to (lover's name), let
his every thought, awake or asleep,
be good thoughts of me.
By my will, so mote it be.

This soap will help keep you in someone's mind even though they are far away. It also makes a good gift to give your traveling lover.

Banishing Negativity Soap

¼ cup cornmeal

2 tablespoons dried vetivert

2 tablespoons dried galangal

3 drops copal oil

4 drops liquid dragon's blood

1¼ cups grated castile soap

If you are not sure of the source of negative energy, you can cover all your bases with an optional idea for making this soap. Write the names of your suspected sources—people and things—on very small scraps of paper. Use the dragon's blood as an ink for doing this. Fold up the scraps of paper as tightly as possible and put them into the soap mixture before it hardens. As you use the soap, and each piece of paper works its way out of the soap, visualize that as being one source of negative energy that you have just overcome and banished. Bury each scrap as it appears to help reinforce the idea that you are grounding harmful energies.

You may wish to burn white candles or frankincense incense while using this soap as you visualize any harm sent to you being taken away down the shower drain as you wash.

Protecting and Warding Soap

¼ cup banana purée

2 tablespoons blackberry juice

6 drops myrrh oil

3 tablespoons grated beeswax

1 cup grated castile soap

With this soap I build a wall,
As wide as me and just as tall;
Shielding me from harmful intent,
Deflecting all negative magick sent.

The banana purée and beeswax are great skin softeners, making you soft on the outside and tough and protected on the inside.

Past Life Soap

½ cup dried hyssop

1 tablespoon dried yarrow

1 teaspoon orris root powder

6 drops lilac oil

1 cup grated castile soap

I open my eyes to second sight,
I seek my other selves this night;
Beyond this shell I look to see,
All the others who are me.

Use this soap prior to magick or meditations whose goal is the viewing of your past lives.

Find a Job Soap

¼ cup grated beeswax

¼ cup grated orange rind

3 drops ginger oil

¾ cup grated castile soap

Suggested food colorings are yellow, gold, or green. Pine incense is another nice addition if you have the space and good ventilation.

Stop Gossip Soap

¼ cup rice bran

2 tablespoons grated beeswax

2 tablespoons dried knotweed or houndstongue

1 drop clove oil

1¼ cups grated castile soap

Fall silent, tongues that wiggle and wag,
By this spell the gossips I gag;
Stilled and hushed be each bitter word,
Harmful gossip no more is heard.

Soap of the Magus

2 tablespoons dried bracken for water power

1 drop jasmine oil

2 tablespoons dried borage for air power

1 drop cumin oil

2 tablespoons alfalfa for earth power

1 drop magnolia oil

2 tablespoons dried coriander for fire power

1 drop allspice oil

1½ cups grated castile soap

Using this soap balances the elements within to help you cultivate your personal magickal powers.

Gel Soaps

Gel soaps are by far the easiest of all soaps to make and can be constructed in one of two ways: one, by placing ingredients in wood ash along with a fatty acid, such as a tropical oil or animal fat, to create a saponifying agent, or soap; or two, by placing the ingredients in a six-ounce container of liquid castile soap or some other neutral-scent liquid with a soaping agent.

The castile soap method is the one I prefer, and it's a formula I will continue to use for magickal shampoos in the next chapter. This olive-oil based soap is all natural, it softens skin, and it is scent neutral, all things that make it a great base for blending magickal oils. These bases can be found at little expense in most drug and discount stores.

The drawback of gel soaps as opposed to solids is that there is less diversity of ingredients since we are mostly limited to essential oils and a few decoctions, which blend well with the liquid soap. Fortunately there are enough choices to cover all conceivable magickal needs, but why limit creativity when solid soaps are easy to make and offer more possibilities?

Gel soaps don't easily go bad but the oils within them can become rancid over the course of several weeks. I like to keep mine in those plastic bottles with the pump tops just for convenience. I usually discard any unused portion after eight weeks, but if you're really working toward the goal of a spell, then you're likely to use all the soap much sooner than that.

Gel soap recipes require no more explanation than this. The chart of actions, desires, and ingredients from earlier in this chapter will guide you as to what oils are best to put in a gel soap for almost any need. Use between six and ten drops of oil total for each eight-ounce bottle of gel soap you make, depending on their strength of scent and irritation potential. Mix well to blend all the soap's ingredients while keeping a clear vision of your goal in mind. A little cornstarch or cream of tartar will thicken the mixture to your taste and add some causticity to increase cleansing power.

Soaks, Splashes, and Scrubs

Soaks are minibaths for the feet and hands that can be done in a pan, bucket, or sink. Splashes are lightly scented waters made from infusions that can be splashed onto your skin as a refresher. They are both portable, convenient, and can soothe and beautify as they work as magickal catalysts.

Soaks should be made as you need them, not in advance. Hands and feet can be soaked in any pan or bowl large enough to place them in with comfort. Do not drink any soak mixture.

Splashes should be kept in bottles that hold no more than eight ounces and have very light lids. They can be carried with you and used when you need a magickal boost, as well as a physical pick-me-up, but should be discarded after six weeks. Never drink any splash or other water product that is without preservatives if it has been sitting unrefrigerated for more than twelve hours or you risk becoming sick. In fact, it's not a good idea to drink your body splashes at all. They are designed for external use only.

A scrub is an exfoliating product, meaning that its goal is to remove the uppermost dead layer of skin from your body. This usually results in a smoother complexion that radiates a healthy, youthful glow. The alpha- and beta-hydroxy acids that have been popular in skin care products in recent years are exfoliators, many taken from natural sources like milk or fruit. The down side to these is that they can cause photosynthetic reactions, meaning the development of rashes or brown spotting when skin is exposed to the sun. They can also irritate and thin the skin, making it more sensitive to cold, wind, and the sun's ultraviolet rays. You should always use a sunscreen when using any exfoliating product.

Cucumber Splash for Invigoration

    5 ounces cucumber decoction
    ½ ounce lemon juice
    2½ ounces spring water
    1 drop sweet pea oil (optional)

See page 18 for decoction instructions. Mix all ingredients in an eight-ounce bottle and use when you need a refresher to help you remain alert or when you need to calm yourself and think clearly. This splash should be applied cold for the best results. Keep it refrigerated if you can.

Beauty Soak for Hands

6 ounces wheat germ oil

1 ounce almond oil

1 ounce tea tree oil

1 package commercial packaged gelatin

Mix ingredients in a pan or bowl large enough to fill with very warm water and place your hands into. The soak will soften skin and cuticles. Enhance the appearance connection of the soak with visualization for attaining general beauty.

Astringent Toner for Refinement

½ teaspoon tea tree oil

½ ounce lemon juice

2 ounces witch hazel

3 ounces apple cider vinegar

2½ ounces rain or spring water

Place all ingredients in an eight-ounce bottle that has a tight cap. A toner should be applied to the face after cleansing. It is a mild astringent that seeks to remove lingering dead skin cells and to rebalance the acid level of the skin. Apply with a cotton ball while visualizing your beauty shining with the refined aura of sophistication and class.

Cash Splash

2 ounces honeysuckle infusion

2 ounces sassafras infusion or tea

2 ounces green tea infusion

2 ounces spring water

A little scent, a little splash,
I find a little needed cash.

See page 18 for infusion directions. Place ingredients in an eight-ounce bottle and use to help bring needed cash when you're in a money emergency.

Right Path Foot Soak

½ cup Epsom salt

½ cup sea salt or baking soda

½ cup cornstarch

½ cup rosemary decoction

¼ cup coconut oil

Staying the course and walking true,
I know now what's right to do.
Higher power, to you I plea,
Keep me on the right path for me.

Place all ingredients in a pan or bowl roomy enough to fill with very warm water and soak your feet. Use this to help keep you walking the right path when you feel you're straying. This can mean straying from your spiritual path, your career path, or any other commitment you wish to keep. It also helps when you're confused about the right path to take and want to keep your feet metaphorically walking in the best direction, but you are unsure what that might be. If you have a God or Goddess to whom you pray, you may use his or her name in place of the words "higher power."

Creativity Boost Splash

2½ ounces clover infusion

½ ounce rosemary infusion

½ ounce cowslip infusion

½ ounce apple juice

1 tablespoon blackberry infusion or tea

3 ounces spring water

Blessed Brighid of Irish fame,
Goddess of all inspirations I may name;
Grant me the blessing of creative mind,
So that my muse I am able to find.

This spell calls on the power of Ireland's famous Goddess of fire, healing, and poetic inspiration, Brighid. If you follow a Christian spiritual path, be aware that Brighid is St. Bridget in modern Catholic Ireland, and you may instead wish to direct your words of power to her.

Place all the ingredients in an eight-ounce bottle that has a tight cap. Use before an exam, job interview, composing music, writing, or embarking on any project requiring creative thought.

Courage Splash

4 ounces sweet pea infusion

2 ounces dill infusion

¼ ounce orange juice

¼ ounce thyme infusion

Place all ingredients in an eight-ounce bottle that has a tight lid. Use when you need to shore up your courage.

Foot Scrub for Protection and Grounding

4 ounces coarse sea salt

2 ounces psyllium seed

1 ounce ground sesame seeds

½ ounce almond or apricot kernel oil

1½ ounces spring water

Place all ingredients in a twelve-ounce jar that has a tight lid and mix until you achieve the consistency of a heavy paste. Add more psyllium if the mixture needs thickening. Scrub feet with a washcloth, sponge, or bath brush to exfoliate rough spots. The psyllium will soothe aches and soften the skin while the salt protects and grounds.

Protection Splash

2 ounces hazel infusion

1 ounce galangal infusion

½ ounce burdock infusion

½ ounce blackberry tea

4 tablespoons holly infusion

½ drop cinnamon oil

4 ounces spring water

A scent, a splash.
A drop, a dash.
Protection, affection.
Warding, direction.
Ever protecting.
Never defecting.
Safety for me,
So mote it be.

Holly has a reputation for protecting anything it touches from lightning strikes. This metaphor can help you protect yourself from unpleasant surprises that strike as fast and unexpectedly as lightning. Place all the ingredients in a twelve-ounce bottle that has a tight lid and use it when either psychic or physical protections are needed.

Love Attracting Splash

3 ounces rose infusion

1 ounce dill infusion

1 ounce columbine or orris root infusion

1 teaspoon vanilla extract

1 ounce spring water

Place all ingredients in an eight-ounce bottle that has a tight lid. Use to attract the magick of love into your life.

four
Lotions and Potions

Beholding beauty with the eye of the mind,
he will be enabled to bring forth, not images
of beauty, but realities.
—Plato

All the women's magazines preach to us that the essence of beauty is wrapped up in having attractive skin. By the modern Western definition of beauty, this means skin free of blemishes that is not too dry and not too oily, possessing an even tone and healthy glow free of damage from sun and stress, and youthful in appearance. That's a pretty unrealistic set of requirements for just looking good.

Contrary to the wild claims of the cosmetic companies, there is no known product you can use that can repair damaged skin. If a product was able to penetrate the deep dermis layer of the skin and affect permanent change, it would be regulated in the United States by the Food and Drug Administration as a drug, not as a cosmetic. The word "cosmetic" refers by definition to appearance, to that which shows only on the most superficial level. The cosmetic companies have repeatedly managed to skirt the laws governing what they can claim their products do and don't do because of the sheer volume of what they produce. With nearly 30,000 cosmetics on the market, and the FDA in possession of data on less than a third of them, it would seem that policing those claims is not a high priority and that extravagant claims will continue to go unchallenged in the name of profit.

Making and Using Magickal Skin Care Products

The skin is not just a covering for the body but an important organ. It is our largest organ, the one that stands between us and the harsh outside world. It should be treated with the care you would give to yourself as a sacred being, a daughter of the Goddess.

Though no known product can permanently change or repair your skin, there are many products that can temporarily improve the appearance and texture of the skin and, for a few hours, help hide flaws like scars and fine lines. And, of course, we can use these magickal lotions to imbue our entire bodies with the energy of a magickal need with or without trying to change the outer appearance of our skin.

Vitamins, collagens, coenzymes, alpha-hydroxy acids, beta-hydroxy acids, and antioxidants have been put into commercial skin care products in the past decade and touted as miracle cures for damaged skin, or at least as methods of slowing the skin-aging process. The truth is that these appear in very minor amounts in most preparations and their effectiveness is unproven.

Collagens are the elastins that give skin its youthful tightness. These fibers break down with age and there's little to be done about it. Collagens are produced naturally in the skin but the molecular structure of those added to lotions is not small enough to penetrate the lower dermis layer and cause any lasting change.

Vitamins and other antioxidants, including coenzymes from meat and nut sources, are excellent guardians of health and immunity when taken internally as recommended by nutritionists, but the effect of their external application on the skin remains unproven. Many of these are moisturizing and can make the skin look and feel better for a while.

Vitamins A, C, and E are popular in skin care products, just as they are in nutritional supplements. Vitamins A and E are fat soluble and harder to mix into creams and lotions. Vitamin C is water soluble, which accounts for its use in a vast number of skin creams. All three have been shown to have an effect on cell regeneration within the body but not necessarily on its surface. Vitamin A is the source of retinol, a popular ingredient in anti-aging creams and lotions.

Soy, rose, celery seed, and other herbs and plants can cause skin to tighten, plump, and look less wrinkled. It certainly doesn't hurt to use these products, and science will likely someday create compounds from these that can penetrate skin and make a real difference. For now, as long as sales of these overhyped products remain high, the cosmetic companies have no incentive to pursue costly research.

Everyone's skin is different and the product that works like a miracle on one person may do nothing for you. You may be allergic to an ingredient or the product may be too greasy or too drying for your skin type. As you've probably discovered in your cosmetic buying already, experimentation is needed to find or devise the formulas that work best for you.

As with all the recipes in this book, you can adapt them for not only powerful magick, but to correspond to your personal beauty regimen by adding ingredients based on your skin's needs. A list of the magickal properties of many oils and herbs appears in the chart on soaps in the previous chapter, so this one will only dwell on the physical manifestations of various ingredients used in magickal lotions.

Desired Lotion Action and Active Ingredients

Antibiotics, Mild. Honey, rosemary oil.

Astringents. Rosemary, witch hazel, cream of tartar, hazelnut oil, grapeseed oil, acacia, rose, lemon juice, apple cider vinegar.

Chapping, Heals. Beeswax, camphor oil, petroleum jelly, cardamom oil, vitamin E oil.

Cleans, Deep. Clay, egg whites, fennel, wintergreen.

Emulsifier. Lecithin.

Exfoliates. Alpha-hydroxy acids, beta-hydroxy acids, salts, witch hazel.

Moisturizers. Avocado, pumpkin, banana, cocoa butter, glycerin, lanolin, wheat germ oil, oatmeal, apricot kernel oil, coconut oil.

Plumps & Tightens. Vitamin E oil, aloe vera, soy, vitamin C, vitamin E, coenzymes, green tea, grapeseed extract, beeswax, carnuba wax.

Redness, Removes. Cornstarch, potato, black alder, tea tree oil, vitamin E oil.

Puffiness, Reduces. Celery seed, potato, buchu, dandelion root.

Preservative. Rosemary (offers some natural protection).

Skin Softeners. Almond oil, coconut oil, oatmeal, mineral oil, honey, hops, barley.

Skin Soothers. Aloe vera, wheat germ, cornmeal, apple cider vinegar, rice bran, honey, psyllium, gelatin.

Sunscreens. Birch bark powder (SPF 8), sesame seed oil (SPF 4), black tea (SPF 2).

Thickeners. Cornstarch, soy paste, nut paste, petroleum jelly, psyllium, oat bran, oatmeal, wheat germ, rice flour, raisin paste, fruit purées, yogurt, milk solids, beeswax, benzoin gum, carnuba wax, aloe vera gel.

Vitamin A Sources. Soy milk and pastes, carrot, pumpkin, kale, cantaloupe, mango, tomato, apricot, milk, sweet potato, squash.

Vitamin C Sources. Red clover, orange, apple, grapefruit, papaya, kiwi, blackberry, honeydew, strawberry, raspberry, lemon, lime.

Vitamin E Sources. Nuts, eggs, parsnip, peach, avocado, wheat germ, almond oil, safflower oil, soy, corn oil, canola oil, olive oil, sunflower seeds.

Wounds, Soothes. Honey, gotu kola, olive oil, aloe vera gel.

Wrinkling, Hides. Any moisturizer, apricot kernel oil.

Magickal Lotions

Lotions can be concocted from scratch using glycerin, milk solids, thickening agents, and emulsifiers. These produce a lotion with a very short shelf life that requires refrigeration. I've tried various scratch lotions and found that, like most of us, I've been spoiled by the richness of commercially produced lotions and don't care for the old-fashioned made-from-scratch potions. I also found these made-from-scratch formulas are more expensive when all the ingredients are added up, and I feel that most of them are just not worth the effort. If you want to experiment with these, then look to the ingredient chart later in this chapter for suggested substances with which to begin experimenting. And don't think you've got it wrong if your end product doesn't look or feel like a "real lotion." This is how most scratch products look and feel.

Here is one scratch lotion base recipe to get you started that so far is the best I've come up with.

Scratch Lotion Base Recipe

- 1 cup aloe vera gel
- ½ cup powdered milk
- ¼ cup grated beeswax or carnuba wax
- ¼ cup glycerin
- 1 teaspoon almond or apricot kernel oil
- 2 tablespoons powdered lecithin

Use caution when placing beeswax, cocoa butter, or other comedogenics on your face. A comedogenic is a cosmetologist's term for a substance that has a high wax content and will clog pores. It is now fashionable to market facial lotions and moisturizers as noncomedogenic to attract buyers concerned about their beauty products creating blackheads and other blemishes.

The easiest way to make magickal lotions that I've found is to purchase a small bottle of inexpensive unscented, noncomedogenic lotion in a drugstore. If you have very dry skin and are not worried about clogging your pores, pure cocoa butter is inexpensive and of low scent, and makes an excellent base.

It is essential that the lotion you use be fragrance free to function as a base for your beauty spells. I've found that the low cost and longer shelf life of these commercially prepared bases allows me to make more than one or two at a time. Oils mix well with these, so they make an excellent base, but the safest and best way to add herbs to lotion bases is to use a tincture.

Tinctures allow you the broadest range of ingredient choices since not every herb you may want to use is produced as an oil, and many essential oils are irritating to the skin or expensive. Tinctures are second to oils in their potency but less irritating, and they distribute the ingredients evenly throughout the lotion base. See chapter 1 for instructions on making tinctures.

To mix the tinctures into their base, you will need to empty the base lotion bottle and use a mixing utensil or your hands to fully work the ingredients together. When it's mixed, transfer it to another jar, preferably a glass one that has a tight lid.

If you have extrasensitive skin, you may want to use a decoction in your lotion base rather than a tincture. The instructions for making decoctions are also given in chapter 1. This method will produce almost no scent but will still allow you to use an herb as a catalyst for magick without risking unpleasant reactions to your products.

You should be cautious about venturing into using herbs that have toxic side effects when ingested, even though you will be using them externally. Many of these are able to penetrate the skin and work their way into the blood stream. Why this never seems to work with substances we want absorbed is beyond me, but that's the way it is. Remember that your skin is an organ just like your heart or lungs, and if you cover it from head to toe with a lotion containing an irritant, toxin, or hallucinogen, you may not be pleased with the results.

Because tinctures have a longer shelf life than either decoctions or essential oils, you can make up to twelve ounces at a time. They should stay fresh for several months, longer if you keep them refrigerated. The recipes shown here are calibrated for six to eight ounces of lotion since these are the standard sizes of commercially prepared lotion bases. If your bottle is larger or smaller, adjust the ingredients proportionally.

Love Attracting Lotion #1

6–8 ounces lotion base

3 tablespoons orange blossom tincture

1 tablespoon palmarosa tincture

1 teaspoon myrtle tincture

1½ teaspoons almond oil (add if your skin is dry)

¼ teaspoon tea tree oil (add if your skin is oily)

1 teaspoon vanilla extract

With the touch of this magickal lotion,
I set the energy of love in motion;
The love made for me can no longer hide,
He seeks me now both far and wide.
Come hither lover, with heart of gold,
Your loving arms around me enfold;
By the power of this sacred potion,
By the power of this magick lotion.
By the power of earth and fire,
By water and air, I seek my desire;
By the power of three times three,
As I will, so mote it be.

Love Attracting Lotion #2

6–8 ounces lotion base

3 tablespoons lemon verbena tincture

2 tablespoons lemon juice

2 tablespoons meadowsweet decoction

2 teaspoons rose petal tincture

3 drops columbine oil

Love Divination Lotion

6–8 ounces lotion base

3 tablespoons apple blossom tincture

2 tablespoons yarrow tincture

2 teaspoons orris root tincture

1 teaspoon flax seed oil

Use this lotion before attempting a divination whose goal is to catch a glimpse of your future mate.

Doctor, lawyer, farmer, sawyer.
Tall or fair, dark steely stare.
Eyes of blue or brown eyes true.
Heart of gold, meek or bold.
Talkative, mild, silent, wild.
Rich or poor, I would see more.
Mirror, show what I would know.
Who is he who's made for me?

Passion Potion #1

6–8 ounces lotion base

2 tablespoons hibiscus tincture

2 tablespoons ginseng tincture

1 teaspoon ginger docoction

You may wish to add a drop or two of ginger oil to this lotion to strengthen the scent.

Passion Potion #2

6–8 ounces lotion base

¼ cup strawberry purée

1 teaspoon fenugreek decoction

2 drops rosemary oil

½ teaspoon tea tree oil (add if your skin is oily)

2 drops coconut oil (add if your skin is dry)

Flying Lotion

6–8 ounces lotion base
- 1 tablespoon parsley tincture
- 1 tablespoon amaranth tincture
- 1 tablespoon mugwort tincture
- 1 tablespoon lemon grass decoction
- 1 teaspoon poplar bark decoction
- 1 drop lilac oil (add if flying to a past life)

Use this lotion to assist you in achieving astral projection or to help use your dreams to step into astral experiences.

Chakra Balancing Lotion

6–8 ounces lotion base
- 1 teaspoon magnolia blossom tincture for the root chakra
- 1 teaspoon sweet pea tincture for the navel chakra
- 1 teaspoon yarrow tincture for the solar plexus chakra
- 1 teaspoon rose petal tincture for the heart center chakra
- 1 teaspoon dandelion tincture for the throat chakra
- 1 teaspoon catnip tincture for the third eye chakra
- 1 teaspoon sandalwood tincture for the crown chakra

The chakras are the seven major energy portals of the body that must remain at least partially open to allow the proper flow of energies to and from yourself and others and between all the operating systems of your body, mind, and spirit. See the diagram in the previous chapter for the chakra locations. This lotion can help stimulate, open, and balance the chakra centers from root to crown.

Healing Lotion

6–8 ounces lotion base
- 3 tablespoons hyssop tincture
- 2 tablespoons carnation tincture
- 1 tablespoon dandelion tincture
- 1 drop camphor or rosemary oil

Air Lotion

6–8 ounces lotion base

2 tablespoons hops

2 tablespoons savory tincture

1 tablespoon mint decoction

1 teaspoon tea tree oil (add if your skin is oily)

1 teaspoon almond oil (add if your skin is dry)

Use this lotion before spells or rituals governed by the element of air to help you attune to its energies.

Fire Lotion

6–8 ounces lotion base

2 tablespoons ginseng tincture

2 tablespoons ginger tincture

2 teaspoons lovage decoction

2 teaspoons green tea infusion

3 drops bayberry oil

Use this lotion before spells or rituals governed by the element of fire to help you attune to its energies.

Water Lotion

6–8 ounces lotion base

2 tablespoons peach purée

2 tablespoons willow bark tincture

2 tablespoons hyacinth tincture

1 tablespoon buchu tincture

Do not use willow bark tincture if you're allergic to aspirin. They contain the same acid base that causes the allergic reaction. Substitute birch bark instead. Use this lotion before spells or rituals governed by the element of water to help you attune to its energies.

Earth Lotion

6–8 ounces lotion base

1 tablespoon honesty (*Lunaria* spp.) tincture

1 tablespoon vetivert tincture

1 tablespoon primrose tincture

1 teaspoon wheat germ oil

Use this lotion before spells or rituals governed by the element of earth to help you attune to its energies. Add a single drop of heady, earthy oil if you like the smell; consider using patchouly or angelica oil.

Fertility Formula

6–8 ounces lotion base

¼ cup banana or pomegranate purée

2 tablespoons bistort tincture

2 teaspoons powdered rice bran or rice flour

½ teaspoon almond oil

¼ teaspoon corn oil

Prosperity Lotion

6–8 ounces lotion base

2 tablespoons melted beeswax (use double boiler)

2 tablespoons honesty (*Lunaria* spp.) decoction

1 tablespoon wheat germ oil

1 drop patchouly or cedar oil (optional)

Abundance of the universe, I call upon you,
Now to fulfill my need that is true;
I ask not for anything beyond what I need,
Prosperity is mine, my call you do heed.

Lunar Lotion

6–8 ounces lotion base

   3 tablespoons gardenia tincture

   2 tablespoons jasmine tincture

   1 tablespoon loosestrife tincture

   1 tablespoon bladderwrack decoction

   1 drop wintergreen or 3 drops sandalwood oil

Use before lunar rituals or spells that use the moon's energy as a catalyst.

Solar Energy Lotion

6–8 ounces lotion base

   2 tablespoons copal tincture

   2 tablespoons lime rind tincture

   2 teaspoons nutmeg or allspice decoction

   2 drops neroli or bergamot oil

Use before solar rituals, sabbat celebrations, or spells that use the sun's energy and archetypes as a catalyst.

Comfort and Consolation Lotion

6–8 ounces lotion base

   2 tablespoons lemon balm tincture

   1 tablespoon marigold tincture

   1 tablespoon skullcap tincture

Protection Lotion

6–8 ounces lotion base

   1 tablespoon agrimony tincture

   1 tablespoon yucca root tincture

   1 tablespoon cardamom tincture

1 tablespoon cumin tincture

⅛ teaspoon liquid dragon's blood

Use this lotion, for either psychic or physical protection, in tandem with commonsense protective measures.

Dream Magick Potion

6–8 ounces lotion base

2 tablespoons mimosa tincture

1 tablespoon bracken tincture

3 drops jasmine or acacia oil

⅛ teaspoon olive oil

Use before going to bed to induce prophetic dreams.

I apply these magickal creams,
To bring to me prophetic dreams;
That I might see and therefore know,
All the night can to me show.
In my sleep throughout this night,
I am blessed with second sight;
Until the rays of dawn come gold,
The future is to me foretold.

Friendship Gel

6–8 ounces lotion base

2 tablespoons aloe vera gel

2 tablespoons passionflower tincture

1 tablespoon meadowsweet tincture

1 tablespoon anise tincture

1 tablespoon knotweed decoction

To make new friends or to strengthen old friendships. Add a little poppy seed to include the bond of fidelity in this lotion.

Overcoming Obstacles

6–8 ounces lotion base

2 tablespoons ginkgo biloba tincture

1 tablespoon black cohosh tincture

1 teaspoon benzoin gum

3 drops sweet pea oil

Psychic Power Potion

6–8 ounces lotion base

1 tablespoon briony tincture

½ tablespoon elder bark tincture

¼ teaspoon bay tincture

2 tablespoons agrimony decoction

You may add a drop or two of cedar, cypress, myrrh, or cardamom oil for scent.

Brain Food

6–8 ounces lotion base

2 tablespoons crushed caraway seeds

1 tablespoon horehound tincture

2 tablespoons sage decoction

You may scent this lotion with a drop or two of rosemary, ginger, or peppermint oil.

Daytime Beauty Lotion

6–8 ounces lotion base

3 tablespoons violet tincture

½ tablespoon lovage tincture

½ teaspoon tamarind tincture

Include one or two drops of violet, geranium, or vanilla oil if you want to add scent.

Evening Beauty Lotion

6–8 ounces lotion base

2 tablespoons lady's mantle tincture

2 tablespoons jasmine tincture

2 drops ylang ylang oil

2 drops sandalwood oil

Gold or silver sparkle

Add a festive touch to this lotion that helps draw the eye by including gold or silver glitter sparkles. You may add a teaspoon of craft glitter or pulverize a small palette of glittering eyeshadow into the lotion. Don't overdo the effect, though—keep it subtle to keep it sensational.

Gold does sparkle, silver shines,
All eyes herein are drawn to mine;
The greatest sensation in the place is me,
Because they see what I want them to see.
Beauty golden under the silvery moon,
To my legendary looks they croon;
Immortalized in their hearts and mind,
Nothing but loveliness in me they do find.

Purification Lotion

6–8 ounces lotion base

2 tablespoons hyssop tincture

2 tablespoons melted carnuba wax

1 teaspoon angelica tincture

1 teaspoon olive oil

You may add a few drops of sandalwood, benzoin, lemon, frankincense, or copal oil for scent.

Spirit Contact Lotion

6–8 ounces lotion base

2 teaspoons mastic decoction

1 teaspoon primrose tincture

1 teaspoon lavender tincture

½ teaspoon hazel tincture

2 tablespoons apple juice

Face Masks

Face masks that both deep clean and soften the skin have been used since ancient times. Depending upon their base and their ingredients they can moisturize and soften, tighten and plump, remove dirt and oils, or make pores appear smaller. The base of the mask is usually a claylike product that coats the face until it dries and adheres to facial impurities. It is then removed either by washing or peeling it away.

One of the best masks ever devised is plain old clay from Mother Earth. The use of clay to soften and deep clean is an ancient beauty practice. This is not advocating that you go outdoors and scoop up a handful of clay-filled dirt to slap on your face. In fact, please don't. The clay in your yard contains dirt, trace minerals, and contaminants you don't want on your skin. Buy kitty litter instead.

You read that right. Many kitty litters are made of pure, 100 percent clay and are—excuse the pun—dirt cheap. Look for the ones that have no chemicals in them to keep down dust and have no clumping agents. The label should read "100 percent pure clay." The other option to obtain pure clay is to buy it in a jar at the cosmetic counter of your local department store, where they will charge you twenty times the price of a huge sack of kitty litter for six ounces of clay in a pretty package with a famous name on the label. Which one would you rather buy?

Commercially prepared masks also have anticaking ingredients and preservatives that allow them to stay fresh in their jars for several months. Your homemade masks have zero shelf-life. Each of the recipes in this section makes enough for one application only. Discard any portion not immediately used.

The one thing these recipes do share with their commercial counterparts is the caution to keep them away from the eye area. The skin around the eyes is too delicate to tolerate most masks without doing more harm than good, and the ingredients can irritate eye tissues or even cause blindness.

Beauty Mask #1

3 egg whites, well beaten

3 tablespoons oatmeal

½ banana purée (use a blender to make)

1 tablespoon honey

Whip the egg whites until they are just starting to stiffen but are not frothy, then mix all the ingredients together in a bowl. This mask is for women with dry skin. Leave it on for at least ten minutes before removing with a warm washcloth.

With clay of earth I make this mask,
Charged with magick to its task;
May the Goddess who dwells in me,
Render me beautiful, so mote it be.

Beauty Mask #2

⅓ cup pure clay

1 teaspoon flaxseed

⅛ teaspoon fenugreek

⅛ teaspoon tea tree oil

⅛ teaspoon cream of tartar

Cream of tarter is a mild astringent but should not be used on the skin of anyone allergic to sulfites. Use powdered cowslip instead or leave it out altogether.

Mix the clay with a little water until it makes a thick paste. Then mix all the other ingredients into the clay, adding a little more water if the mixture becomes too thick to blend.

continued . . .

This mask is for women with oily skin who are prone to having blackheads. Leave it on for ten minutes before removing with a warm washcloth.

Empowered be this mask,
Charged to its task;
Beauty shines from me,
And so mote it be.

Redness Reducing Mask

¼ cup pure clay

1 tablespoon mashed potatoes

⅛ teaspoon borage

⅛ teaspoon cornstarch

6 drops tea tree oil

Mix the clay with a little water until it makes a thick paste. Then mix all the other ingredients into the clay, adding a little more water if the mixture becomes too thick to blend.

This mask was not created with magickal uses in mind, but that does not mean there aren't any. You could certainly use the potato as a catalyst for grounding and stabilizing yourself when you feel frazzled or anxious.

Peeling Off Your Old Life

2 tablespoons pure clay

1 small package gelatin (about 3 tablespoons)

1 egg white, beaten

1 tablespoon rice bran

Whip the egg whites until they are just starting to stiffen but are not frothy, then mix all the ingredients together in a bowl. The egg symbolizes rebirth and the gelatin and clay are earth-governed for stability and grounding as you start a fresh life. The rice is also a fertility symbol: fertile earth for growing a new you.

For this mask use plain gelatin, not a commercial food product containing sugars and dyes. The gelatin will allow you to peel the mask off once it has dried rather than wash it off. As you peel it away be sure to hold a clear visualization of it removing all the unwanted elements of your life and starting anew.

I have seen red ochre used in these types of masks, but I don't recommend it. Ochre is a natural iron oxide that was used in ancient Egypt to represent blood in rituals. It was used to cover the bodies of the dead or sick to ensure healing and resurrection. Its drawback is that it stains the skin badly; not red as you might expect, but yellow.

> *As if in a chrysalis I have formed a new me,*
> *Like the butterfly I emerge to be all I can be;*
> *My old self is gone and a new one is born,*
> *A better me emerges like a rose without thorn.*

Love Attracting Mask

2 tablespoons pure clay

1 egg white, beaten

1 teaspoon fig purée

1 teaspoon avocado purée

Whip the egg whites until they are just starting to stiffen but are not frothy, then mix all the ingredients together in a bowl. Wear while visualizing a new love coming into your life. This mask works especially well after performing a bath or shower love spell.

Job Seeker's Mask

2 tablespoons pure clay

2 egg whites, beaten

2 tablespoons soy meal

2 tablespoons unflavored yogurt

Whip the egg whites until they are just starting to stiffen but are not frothy. Then mix all the ingredients together in a bowl. Use before going job hunting to gain confidence and to project an air of competence to your interviewer.

Healing Mask

¼ cup pure clay

1 tablespoon cornmeal

⅛ teaspoon green tea

⅛ teaspoon agrimony

Mix the clay with a little water until it makes a thick paste. Then mix all the other ingredients into the clay, adding a little more water if the mixture becomes too thick to blend.

Skin Balancing Mask

1 small package gelatin

1 tablespoon pure clay

1 tablespoon cucumber purée

1 teaspoon mashed cantaloupe

¼ teaspoon crushed sunflower seeds

⅛ teaspoon powdered marjoram

⅛ teaspoon dried linden

⅛ teaspoon dried mint leaves

This is a mask to use for the pure pleasure of it. The linden cools, the mint tingles, and the sunflower seeds are both moisture-rich and help cleanse your face. This mask is more invigorating than relaxing, so avoid using it at bedtime if you want to wind down for the day.

Facial Steams

Prepackaged face masks have made the more complicated and time-consuming facial steams less popular. About the only time you see someone hanging over a vaporizer or steaming kettle is during cold and flu season, when the user is desperately trying to clear their stuffed-up head. This image has cast the once-popular facial steam in a less than romantic guise.

Steams are great for cleaning out pores, removing oil buildup and blackheads, softening skin, and improving facial circulation. Some very expensive spas and salons charge the proverbial queen's ransom for the privilege of hanging over a steaming pot of the same herbs you can use at home, where you have the added advantage of being able to empower them to your magickal will beforehand.

The easiest way to steam your face is to have a private sauna available where you can have the incense for your facial burning near you and all the controlled steam you want encircling your body. When you stop laughing, you can read on and learn other ways to make a facial steam work. And to anyone who has that private sauna . . . the rest us don't want to hear about it.

If you own a vaporizer—the kind that is used in winter to help you breathe when you have the flu—and the instructions say that it's permissible to place aromatic items in a small tray next to the steamer opening made for this purpose, then this is ideal. If your vaporizer's instructions say not to put anything near the steam opening, then trust that they know what they're talking about and either use another method or buy a different vaporizer. Don't add anything foreign to the water itself as it can only result in one of three outcomes: failure of the unit to produce steam, clogging or breaking of the vaporizer, or an electrical fire.

The other way to get the steam you need is by hanging your head over a tea kettle or pot of water simmering on the stove top. The advantage of this method is that you can put anything into the water you blasted well choose. The disadvantage is that it's not portable and you can't sit on your sofa and relax as you steam your face.

Whether you use a vaporizer, simmering pot, or tea kettle, place a towel over your head to make a tent to help trap the steam around your face. Be mindful that steam burns occur quickly and are among the worst type of burns. Don't get too close to the source of the steam. You want warmth and moisture, not scalding heat, which can also cause broken capillaries to appear. Don't wear bracelets or neck chains or anything else that could catch on the pot or kettle and pull the water down over you. This would result in the sort of burn that would require emergency medical treatment and—yipes!—would really wreck your spell. Ten to twenty minutes under the steam tent is long enough for both the spell and the beauty treatment to work.

Beauty Facial Steam #1

3 cups spring water
¼ cup hops or barley
¼ teaspoon dried feverfew
⅛ teaspoon dried spearmint
   Pinch dried coltsfoot

Steaming, streaming, ever-seeming—
Beautiful all are ever me deeming.

This facial steam is best for dry skin that needs moisture. Wash your face afterward with a mild soap and then pat it dry. Moisturize as usual.

Beauty Facial Steam #2

3 cups spring water
¼ cup lemon juice
¼ teaspoon dried acacia
¼ teaspoon dried comfrey
¼ teaspoon fennel

This facial steam is best for skin that is oily and prone to blackheads. Clean your face afterward with a mild astringent soap and wipe down with a cotton-ball that has been soaked in witch hazel or apple cider vinegar.

Steam for a Steamy Romance

3 cups spring water
¼ cup dried rose hips
½ teaspoon dried rosemary
1 drop peppermint oil

Love and passion everlasting,
Come to me, whose heart is fasting;
Come in love, my world to transform,
Come with the intensity of a summer storm.

Healing Facial Steam

3 cups spring water

1 teaspoon dried spearmint leaves

½ teaspoon dried rosemary

⅛ teaspoon dried eucalyptus (not the oil)

⅛ teaspoon feverfew

Powers of healing and wellness I call,
Break through the brick of sickness's wall;
Penetrate my being as I steam my face,
Remove all taint of illness's trace.

If you're going to use steam to treat a cold or flu, you might as well add some magickal effort to boost the process. The only time this would be contraindicated is if you have a fever; then you should not be steaming your head with anything. Try a cool healing bath instead.

Relaxing Steam

3 cups spring water

1 teaspoon dried lavender

¼ teaspoon sage

⅛ teaspoon powdered allspice

2 drops cardamom oil

This is a steam for the pure enjoyment of it. The aromas should relax you and help you sleep.

Massage Oils

Massage oils are a great way for two magickal partners to have some quality time together while crafting their spells, especially if they are also romantic partners. There is little that feels quite so pleasurable as having someone you trust and are sexually attracted to kneading your muscles with a slow and steady hand.

Massage oils in and of themselves serve two functions, and in magick they serve three. They make it easy for the hands to move over the surface of the skin without dragging or burning, and they provide aromatherapy in the form of scent, which can trigger sexual or romantic feelings. Used in magick they provide the catalyst for any spellwork the two of you wish to do.

The art of sensual massage has grown in popularity and several books are now available on the topic. The key to making it work is allowing yourself both to enjoying giving and receiving this pleasure without feelings of anxiousness. You should each spend at least fifteen minutes on your partner's body without feeling pressured to do more or less. This allows you both to be able to fully engage in the experience without feeling he or she is making you do something you don't enjoy doing or are not going to get anything for in return.

Have your partner lie on his or her stomach and slowly knead the major muscle groups in the upper back, upper and lower legs, and buttocks. Use steady pressure but don't feel you have to press hard or wear out your hands. The oil will allow you to move freely over the skin and will heat slightly under the friction of your touch.

Though sex magick has grown in popularity it is unnecessary for making a massage-oil spell work. The simple act of caressing one another can raise energy that the two of you can focus on a goal you share. These oils can be used alone or in addition to any other spell whose efficacy you wish to boost with some added energy.

If you find you become too relaxed or too absorbed in each other's presence to focus on your goal, you can borrow a page from the sex magician's manual and add to your magick a visual symbol. This symbol will give your subconscious minds something to focus on without having to consciously connect with the magical goal during the more intimate moments of your mutual massage session.

To make a symbol, you must first agree with your partner on the goal and write it out word for word so there is no chance of miscommunication. Together you will then need to create a visual image of that goal. Don't try to be fancy. You don't need artistic talent, just a simple symbol on which you both can agree. For example, a spell for protection might need no more than a pentacle or large *X* to trigger your subconscious to remember what it's working toward. A pentacle is a pentagram, or five-pointed star, with its apex pointing up, which is surrounded in a circle. From ancient times it has symbolized totality, protection, and mastery of the divine and of the magician over the elements that make up the universe. The pentacle has been adopted as the symbol of the modern Wiccan tradition of Witchcraft.

Spend time gazing at the symbol before you begin the magickal massage and allow yourselves to make a deep connection between this image and the desired goal. This step must be done enough so that, over time, this symbol even invades your dreams as a representation of your goal. This is how you know it is working. Place copies of the symbol where it can be seen from any place in the area in which you will be massaging one another. As your eyes fall upon it, your subconscious mind will be triggered to work toward the goal while you enjoy the massage. Just keep in mind that this symbol method of triggering your magick is not an easy out. You must put a lot of effort into connecting with the symbol beforehand for its energy to work for you while you focus on other things.

What follows are three base recipes for massage oil with some suggestions for scent and scent combinations that will help trigger magick without irritating your skin. Make no more than four ounces at a time as they do not keep well. Six-ounce bottles made from dark glass with tight lids are recommended. Refrigerating massage oils makes them much too cold to apply to bare skin and defeats much of their purpose.

Massage Oil Base #1

2 ounces almond oil

1½ ounces apricot kernel oil

This oil is best on dry skin.

Massage Oil Base #2

2 ounces vitamin E oil

½ ounce corn oil

½ ounce witch hazel

1 teaspoon tea tree oil

This oil is best on oily skin.

Massage Oil Base #3

2 ounces olive oil

1 ounce canola or safflower oil

½ ounce wheat germ oil

This oil is best on normal skin that is not prone to breaking out.

Other Magickal Oil Ideas

The following are recipe suggestions for ingredients to add to the massage oil bases that provide results both from their aroma and their power as magickal catalysts. Experiment with your favorite nonirritating essential oils and extracts to find recipes whose scent you find pleasing and whose magick works for you and your partner. Be sure to keep any product containing essential oil away from the eyes and from tender genital tissue, where it can cause unpleasant burning and itching.

To Create Lust

½ teaspoon anise extract

3 drops ginger oil

For Strengthening Love

½ teaspoon vanilla extract

3 drops jasmine oil

1 drop rose oil

For Relaxing

3 drops bayberry oil

1 drop bergamot oil

1 drop linden blossom (optional)

For Enhancing Spiritual Feelings

4 drops sandalwood oil

2 drops ylang ylang oil

2 drops geranium oil

For Creating Wealth

3 drops orange or neroli oil

2 drops clary sage oil

1 drop nutmeg oil

To Strengthen Fidelity

¼ teaspoon cherry extract

3 drops cypress oil

To Enhance Fertility

½ teaspoon almond extract

2 drops patchouly oil

For Protection

½ teaspoon orange extract

1 drop clove oil

1 drop allspice oil

For Help in Healing

3 drops sandalwood oil

1 drop carnation oil

½ drop rosemary oil

To Invigorate

2 drops angelica oil

2 drops vetivert oil

To Stimulate All the Senses

3 drops juniper oil

1 drop peppermint oil

The Infamous Flying Ointment

Most books on the history of magick or Witchcraft address flying ointments, those noxious concoctions of goo that reputedly covered the naked body and helped the user achieve the state of altered consciousness and heightened awareness we know as astral projection or out-of-body travel.

The astral plane is conceptualized as a world both paralleling and interpenetrating our own, remaining unnoticed by us in our normal waking state of consciousness. This world is no less real than our own, it just has a different set of rules and different inhabitants. As an intrepid traveler once said, "It's a nice place to visit, but I wouldn't want to live there." The astral world is the unseen world in which all thought is first formed and where magick first takes shape. Magick performed on the astral plane is potent and one step closer to manifestation than many other types of magick, yet it remains an advanced art requiring practice to master.

When we astral project, we send our consciousness to this otherworld. Whether any part of us actually leaves the body is not clear. We continue to debate this point ad nauseum and continue to refer to this art as both an "out-of-body experience" and as "inner-plane work," all of which underscore our inadequate efforts to precisely define this state of being.

The flying ointments that have become infamous over the centuries contain narcotics and other hallucinogens that alter the consciousness with no concerted effort on the part of the magician. Others contain toxic substances that alter the consciousness by creating dangerous physiological responses in the body, including the constriction of blood vessels, the production of histamines, and the dual and deadly combination of lowering blood pressure while raising the heart rate. They are literally poisoning the body. The person using them is more likely to be having a near-death experience than to be engaging in any productive activity on the astral plane.

There has been a theory bandied about the Pagan community for years that hypothesizes that these ingredients were not standard in the flying ointments of old Europe but were merely reported as such during Witch trails when the person confessing them was under torture. The idea was that the accused knew that the accusers would not be able to resist experimenting and would likely die in the attempt.

I once gave great credence to this theory but have had reason to change my opinion. Anthropologists studying native tribes in remote areas of the upper Amazon, almost untouched by the outside world, have found many of them use hallucinogens in spiritual ritual. If indigenous peoples use these hallucinogens for spiritual practice, it stands to reason that it might have also been a practice in Europe. But this still does not mean using them is a good idea. Many natives are addicted to these substances and, as a result, are unable to function well in their everyday world.

Without getting into issues of moral, ethical, or legal behavior I will state only that achieving an altered state of consciousness should be a skill any practicing magician can call upon at will. Help in doing this should not be needed on a regular basis. However, altered states share much in common with sleep patterns, and we all know that sometimes, for no discernible reason, sleep just will not come. The same is true with altered states. Sometimes it just won't happen. At that point you will have to make the choice for yourself of how much help you seek and of what kind. Just know the risks.

Keep in mind that there is a difference between controlled hallucinogens that can serve medical functions and poisons that push users to the edge of death. Even the so-called "mild poisons" like mistletoe or wormwood can produce unpleasant results if used by someone unfamiliar with their effect. On the plus side, most so-called mild poisons are not addictive. Hallucinogens in carefully administered amounts shift consciousness and do not immediately threaten physical existence, though they are addictive. Though I don't advocate the use of either, you should be aware of this distinction between them.

A third choice for altered state assistance are herbal teas that help slow the mind, which include sedatives such as catnip and valerian. A weak infusion of either steeped with mint to cut the bitter taste is all that's needed to use them. I feel this is the best substance to turn to when you need a little help in achieving your magickal state of mind. Herbal teas are the least addictive and their resulting effects don't run over you like a rampaging steamroller. They assist your shift in consciousness rather than take it over.

Two common additives in these old flying ointments that made them even more unpleasant to use were lard and lamp black. Lard was commonly used as the base for mixing the herbal ingredients into an ointment. It is messy and smelly. Today's magician is more likely to select petroleum jelly or even an unscented lotion base. An astral projection lotion recipe appears earlier in this chapter for those who are interested in this alternative.

Lamp black is the carbon that collects on the inside of glass-encased candles as their wicks burn. This was reputedly used to help disguise Witches as they gathered in secret under the cover of darkness, though there are problems with this theory. If Witches were meeting via astral projection, then they would not need to leave their homes and would not need to be disguised. If they were already at a coven gathering, they would not be hiding anything by blackening themselves. If they were in the process of skulking through the woods on their way to a coven meeting, then they would not need to be wearing a flying ointment.

There are numerous books available that teach the art of astral projection if you are unfamiliar with it and want to learn. There are so many different concepts of the art of projecting, so many different methods of doing so, and so many variations of mental imagery that you can be sure one will work for you. Just be aware that effort and experimentation will be required to be successful, no matter what method or methods eventually work best for you. Books you might investigate are J. H. Brennan's *Astral Doorways* (Aquarian Press, 1986), Robert Cockrell's *The Study and Practice of Astral Projection* (University Press, 1966), D. J. Conway's *Flying Without a Broom* (Llewellyn, 1995), Robert Monroe's *Journeys Out-of-Body* (Anchor, 1977), John Perkins' *PsychoNavigation* (Destiny Books, 1990), Scott Rogo's *Leaving the Body* (Prentice Hall, 1983), or my own *Astral Projection for Beginners* (Llewellyn, 1998) in which I outline six different methods of astral projection.

Each of the recipes in this chapter makes enough ointment for one person to apply before a single astral projection attempt. If you wish to make ointment for more than one person, simply multiply the proportions accordingly. Keep in mind before applying that these ointments are very messy and they will wreck clothes and carpets and could irritate your skin. Blend it well into your skin for the easiest use and least mess.

Flying Ointment #1

¼ teaspoon parsley

¼ teaspoon mugwort

⅛ teaspoon powdered orris root

⅛ teaspoon chicory

Pinch of gotu kola

Pinch of eyebright

1 ounce petroleum jelly

Flying Ointment #2

¼ teaspoon mugwort

⅛ teaspoon amaranth

⅛ teaspoon mastic

Pinch of lemongrass

Pinch of powdered marjoram

1 ounce petroleum jelly

Leg-Shaving Lotion for Great Gams

No matter where your feminist sensibilities place you in the debate of should you or shouldn't you with regard to hair removal, the fact remains that, for many women, shaving the legs is a daily event. We may not look forward to it. We may wish we'd never started doing it. We may even resent feeling compelled to do so, but many of us do it just the same. Like any beauty or grooming process, shaving the legs is yet another ritual we can turn into a magickal spell to enhance personal attraction.

We are all aware of the existence of "leg men," male onlookers who are sexually attracted to women with legs of a specific shape, length, and girth. The evolved part of our brains criticizes this behavior as dehumanizing us via the fetishization of our female body parts. The primitive part of our brains wants to make those fetishized parts as alluring as possible to the male on the prowl for a mate. This male impulse, and the female ambivalence toward it, may be part of that primitive pursuit of the fertile partner that some scientists believe underlies the relentless quest for beauty.

Magick won't tone and tighten your legs. Only a good lower-body workout will get you those. Magick can enhance the physical appeal of your legs to others by using catalysts, visualization, and words of power. To back up this magick in the physical world you should not only exercise—for health as well as beauty—but dress to flatter your body type. Legs that are excessively thin or heavy do not have universal appeal in short skirts. While you should never let the opinions of others dictate your fashion choices on a daily basis, thinking about those opinions can be a big boost to an appearance spell such as this one.

Dark stockings, shoes without high rises and ankle straps, and wearing stockings and shoes in the same shade all increase your vertical line and make your legs appear longer and thinner. Hemlines today are so versatile that you can choose the ones in which you look best without sacrificing fashion. Unless your legs are very thin, try to avoid those hemlines that hit you midcalf. This is not flattering on most women because it creates a horizontal line at the widest part of the leg and this adds visual weight.

Magickal Leg-Shaving Lotion

3 ounces cocoa butter

1 ounce plain yogurt

1 ounce honey

½ ounce lemon or lime juice

3 tablespoons glycerin

4 drops violet or rose oil

1 drop rosemary oil

You may want to consider using an electric mixer to blend your shaving lotion, since allowing it to be whipped for several minutes will soften and aerate the cocoa butter. This makes it easier to apply, allows it to go further, and makes it less likely to clog your razor.

Place the mixture in an eight-ounce jar that has a very snug lid. This will keep about eight days when not refrigerated. I do not recommend refrigeration for shaving lotions. The formula gets too cold and then is uncomfortable to apply. The resulting chill also raises goosebumps which, when shaved, produce red, irritated skin.

Slather the shaving cream onto your legs while visualizing them becoming longer, sleeker, and more appealing to everyone who sees them. Shave with slow, deliberate strokes. Try to think of this not as a chore, but as a opportunity in which you—not your onlookers—are in the power position. (Yes, I know this is the hardest part. I hate shaving too.)

As you shave, go over and over these words of power:

I'm a golden girl with golden gams,
Hard as horses, soft as lambs,
Sturdy as oaks and pretty as a rose,
With sexy legs from hips to toes.

five
Hair Magick

There is no excellent beauty that hath
not some strangeness in the proportion.
—Francis Bacon

Every culture, haute culture, subculture, and counterculture, in every time and every place, has used hairstyle, color, and adornment to make personal statements about the social, economic, and political orientation of the wearer. Perhaps more so than the fashions garmenting the body, those worn on the head leave the most lasting impressions. When we think of Marie Antoinette, we get a clear image of her hair piled several feet high above her forehead. We can't separate our mental image of George Washington from the powdered white wig he wore. When asked to describe someone from the punk culture, we usually talk about the rainbow-hued hair before the black leather clothes and body piercings.

Many people are unaware that the hair adorning our heads has been tapped for its magickal potential since deep into prehistory. Folk legends and myths bombard us with tales of its power, and modern humanity has referred to hair as "a woman's crowning glory." The Judeo-Christian Bible relates the story of Samson, a mighty warrior whose power was bound up in his hair that, when cut by his lover Delilah, rendered him powerless in battle. The fearsome Goddess Medusa had hair made of living snakes. The Irish deities known as the Tuatha de Danaan are described as tall and golden-haired, fair and shining like the sun.

Hair has been used as both a keepsake from and an offering to the dead. As one of the last remnants of the physical body to decay, hair has been shorn to show deep mourning and it has been placed on altars honoring ancestor spirits. The Victorians popularized the making of keepsakes from locks of hair, which were carried in lockets or woven into distasteful mosaics along with the hair of others before being mounted in a frame.

Brushes and Braids

Folk beliefs concerning hair are still with us today. Most of them originated in western Europe and came to North America with the English and Scottish immigrants who settled the southern Appalachian region. Other folk legends came from the Middle East, where hair was believed to hold part of the soul and could be used to curse the person who lost it. Many older Jewish women will burn hair taken from a comb or brush rather than risk throwing it away where just anyone could find it.

In many places around the world, the hair of a child is not cut until that child attains a specific age, such as age three. This is so that the cutting of his hair will not weaken him, like Samson in the biblical myth. The long hair was also considered a good disguise for a defenseless child. The androgynous look was said to keep wandering spirits from stealing him or her away.

Talismans made of hair and nail clippings have been used both to curse and to deflect curses. Birds and bats that become entangled in the hair have been believed to bring omens of death or ill fortune.

Hair has been used as healing tool. It has been shaved to cure fever, and nailed to trees or buried to stop a curse or prevent illness.

Using a Strand of Hair as a Pendulum

A single strand is sometimes used as a divination tool. If you have hair more than a few inches long, you almost always have a ready pendulum when you need an oracle in a hurry. Tie onto that strand a ring or pendant so it can be suspended from the hair while you ask yes and no questions. In a process known as pendulum reading, the movement of the object being suspended from the hair determines the answer to the question. Clockwise and up-and-down motions are usually interpreted as positive or affirmative answers, while counterclockwise and side-to-side motions are usually interpreted as negative answers.

Reflections of Your Future Love

Another divination to try if your hair is at least shoulder length will allow you to see a vision of your future mate. You will also need a mirror and a hairbrush.

This divination is believed to have originated in England but has been popular in the southern Appalachian Mountains of the United States. Just before sundown, sit in front of the mirror and begin combing your hair. Brush it slowly and deliberately for exactly 100 strokes. Counting has always worked well to slow the mind and make it receptive. As you brush and count, allow yourself to be lulled into an altered state of consciousness that will open you up to psychic visions of the future.

You may want to use a chant or quatrain to help you focus on the goal of this divination as you brush your hair. Try something such as:

The western horizon the sun now cloaks,
As I brush one hundred strokes;
Pray I see, and know no fear,
My lover's face as in this mirror I peer.

As you near the one hundredth stroke of your brush, lean forward slightly and brush your hair down over your face. Peer through the veil of your hair into the mirror to catch of glimpse of your future mate.

An interesting side note to this spell is that, in Appalachia, it is believed that this divination should never be extended beyond sunset or the reflection the young woman sees in the mirror will be that of her own funeral.

Binding with Braids

The binding power of hair was an accepted fact in old Celtic societies. Celtic women held a status equal to that of men in their culture. Women owned land, chose their own sexual and marriage partners, served as warriors and priestesses, and were clan leaders and queens. Yet Celtic women were obliged to come to the altar of marriage with their hair unbound. This proved to her mate and all who witnessed their joining that she was not using the magick of her braided hair to ensnare her man.

The drawback of any type of binding magick is that most of it crosses that fuzzy gray line of manipulative magick. It can also bind things to you that you didn't expect. An old Witch's adage teaches, "As ye bind, so are ye bound." The creation of our spells is as circular as the cycles of the seasons. What we do to craft the spell here in the world of form becomes manifest in the unseen realms, which is then brought through our magick into the world of form, which began with what we did to craft the spell, and so on and so on. These "as above, so below; as within, so without" scenarios known to magicians make it reasonable to assume that when we create something that binds we risk binding more than we bargained for.

When you have the man you want madly in love with you, and want to keep him that way, prepare yourself to make magick and begin to wind your hair into a slow tight braid. Start with three evenly divided sections of hair that you see as representing you, your lover, and the union of your love.

Visualize your lover and all that is positive about your relationship as you weave your hair. Also keep in mind the sacred imagery of Celtic artwork, which features braids and interwoven knots. This symbolizes the unity of all spirits through the maze of existence and, as in the three braids, employs the Celtic sacred number three.

As you braid your hair, chant over and over:

> *(Full name of lover) must now be,*
> *Ever, always, in love with me.*

When you reach the end of the braid you may tie it off with any item you choose, but since this is a magickal act rather than a utilitarian one, try to find something that speaks to your mind of a connection to your spell's goal. If you use only a simple rubber band, at least try to have it in a color that makes magickal sense to you. For example, use red for passion or blue for fidelity. Better yet, find something with a flower motif, such as a rose for love, or a barrette with knotwork. Make this as much as magickal object as any oil, wand, or candle you own and use it only for this spell.

Further seal your spell with words of power that call upon the Celtic God of love, Aengus MacOg, as you tie off your braid:

> *Entwined in braid my spell is cast,*
> *My love to me is bound steadfast;*
> *By Aengus MacOg, our God of love,*
> *As below, so above.*
> *Entwined in braid my spell is cast,*
> *(Full name of lover) and I handfast*;*
> *Three strands that bind his heart to me,*
> *As I will, so mote it be.*

*A Pagan term from Western Europe, "handfast" means to marry, sometimes as in a trial marriage of a year and a day. Modern Witches, Wiccans, and many Pagans still use this term when referring to a wedding or bonding ceremony in which a commitment whose terms have been agreed on beforehand and for a specific time period is publicly made. This custom is the source of the modern phrase "asking her hand in marriage."

Energy Brushing

There are many ways to raise magickal energy. One method that is usually overlooked by the solitary practitioner is the act of brushing one's hair. It doesn't matter how long or short your hair is; if you can run a brush through it, you can brush up some major magickal energy for any imaginable need or desire. This is especially true on cold, dry days when the brush will stir up static electricity and you can feel your hair crackle with a power all its own.

Brushing can be hard on your hair and, if done too often or with a rough hand, can cause breakage. Be gentle when you brush for magick. Brushing vigorously or quickly will not raise any more energy than will doing it slowly and gently.

As you brush, visualize any magickal need and, if you like, recite your words of power to help keep you focused. When you feel you have raised all the energy you can, put your brush down and run your hands and forearms over your hair to smooth it down. As you do this, visualize the energy built up in it being released toward your goal.

If you find yourself halfway through this spell and change your mind about going through with it, wet your hands and rub them over your head to reverse the electric charge and ground the energy before it is released.

Brushing Up Psychic Protection

Another excellent use of energy brushing is psychic protection. The energy you build can be woven into a shield of protection that can deflect negative intent or harmful magick that has been directed your way. Visualize the energy you brush up forming into a shield or egg around you that sparkles with static electricity and deflects negativity. You may either visualize it being sent into Mother Earth to be safely grounded or you may want to see it being returned to its sender. Just be sure not to visualize a specific person as the sender just in case you're wrong. You don't want to chance being the source of unwarranted negative magick.

Magickal Shampoos

When you think about how shampoo works and how it not only flows over the head that connects us to other worlds and beings, but how it flows gently over the body as it's rinsed away, it's amazing that it's not employed in spellcraft more often. You have the power of water, of scent, and the imagery of immersing yourself in the spell both literally and figuratively.

You have two choices when employing magickal shampoos: one, you can actually create a product that cleans the hair and combine your hair washing with your magickal goal; or two, you can make a shampoo that is solely magickal in its properties and use it before or after—or in place of—shampooing for cleansing. The latter is actually not a shampoo but a rinse. If you prefer using a rinse to a shampoo, simply remove the soap agent—usually castile soap—and replace it with spring water. You may use a rinse either before or after using a conditioner.

When you make magickal shampoos you should always start with good water. Don't use tap water that contains chlorine, fluoride, or other contaminants. Invest a dollar or two in spring water or water from some other purified source. These can be found in almost any grocery store. Avoid using distilled water, which has had the life energy processed out of it. Collecting dew and rainwater to use are also possibilities, but please reconsider this if you live in an area whose rainfall is dubbed "acid rain"—one that is laced with contaminants by being downwind of industries that have polluted the air above them.

When making magickal shampoos you will need to start from scratch. Oils and other magickal catalysts do not mix well in commercial shampoos the way they do in lotions or gel soaps. They usually create an unpleasant smell or a result that is not attractive. They can gunk up and become thick or suddenly become runny and leave a tacky residue on the hair.

Your homemade shampoos will not contain preservatives like your commercial brands, and they will not keep as long, especially in the warm dampness of your bathroom. Make no more than six to eight ounces at a time even if you're a frequent shampooer. Toss out the shampoo if it becomes discolored or starts to smell rancid, just as you would with any magickal oil blend or other cosmetic product.

Plastic bottles are the safest storage containers for bath products, but products keep better in glass bottles with tight lids. I admit to occasionally opting for the safety factor by using plastic storage for things I use in the bathroom. Glass shards in bare feet are not magickal. When I decide to forgo glass, I buy only high quality, wide mouthed, plastic jars that are opaque and thicker than your usual shampoo bottle. This means that I open a wide-mouthed jar and dip my fingers in the shampoo to get it out, rather than use the squeeze bottles we're used to using for shampoo products. Also, insist on snug screw-on lids for all your homemade shampoo containers.

Any magickal shampoo I make without preservatives, or whose composition and smell can be altered by heat and light, usually stays in my refrigerator between uses. Granted that the image of fishing my shampoo out from behind a carton of milk may not be the most magickal, but even less magickal is going through all the preparations of mind and body for spellcrafting only to have it ruined because I just placed a glob of rancid liquid on my head that I can't wait to wash off.

As you did with your bath salt and oil blends, you should always keep records when blending your shampoos. Use oils sparingly, as they can grease up your hair quickly and, in some cases, irritate the scalp.

Homemade shampoos are usually gentler than detergent-based commercial products, but they may not clarify as well. The addition of a little baking soda can help remove the buildup of other shampoos and styling products, but it is an abrasive that should not be used on a regular basis. A half-teaspoon placed in a six-ounce mixture that is used once a week is plenty.

If you want your shampoo to serve as a cleansing agent as well as a magickal one, you will need a detergent or soap component. Avoid using borax as it makes a good soap base but is too harsh for your hair. Powdered soap can also irritate lungs. Soap flakes are one choice, but this can sometimes be too drying for hair. Some herbs are natural astringents that work well on oily hair, such as witch hazel, but are too harsh when used daily. Castile soap is the gentlest choice. It can be bought in liquid form so that it doesn't require melting for shampoos, but it too can sometimes be overly moisturizing for oily hair and can weight it down.

Sulfonated castor oil is not only a soap but it adds a richness to shampoo and increases its ability to soften hair. Used in soft water, it will also allow you to work up a real fine mess of lather. Two teaspoons is the most you would need to add to any shampoo recipe. Reduce castile soap to only one ounce and use spring water to make the rest of your shampoo base when working with sulfonated castor oil.

Rosemary and jojoba both remove the sebum that can clog the hair's roots and produce oils. Jojoba and its cousin plants have even been shown to have some beneficial effect on hair loss since sebum can clog the scalp and block new growth. When I lived in Texas I was given a cousin plant of jojoba by a curandera, or folk healer, to help prevent hair loss caused by a medication I was taking. It worked well enough that I stopped panicking when I looked at all the lost hair accumulating in my comb every morning. Unfortunately, this is also when I learned my first lesson about the clogging effect of loose herbs in drain pipes.

Converting Oils to Decoctions

If you feel oils are too strong for your magickal shampoos, then try making a decoction from dried herbs and using that as your base rather than using essential oils. This is usually my preference anyway. Chapter 1 will take you through the steps of making decoctions.

To translate the oil recipes you find here or elsewhere into a decoction simply interpret the oil drops as "parts" of the whole recipe, then use a half teaspoon of the dried herb for each single part. Do this for the oils only and leave other items as they appear. For example:

> 3 drops lavender oil = 1½ teaspoons dried lavender
>
> 2 drops orange oil = 1 teaspoon grated orange rind
>
> 1 drop rosemary oil = ½ teaspoon dried rosemary
>
> 1 cup rose water = 1 cup rose water
>
> ¼ teaspoon cornmeal = ¼ teaspoon cornmeal

Place the items—minus any bases like liquid castile soap—in a saucepan and simmer for at least ten minutes. Be sure not to let herbs settle at the bottom and become scorched. When the decoction has boiled down to about half its original volume, remove it from the heat and allow it to cool. Filter it through a cheesecloth into a glass bottle for use in your shampoo blend.

Desired Shampoo Action and Active Ingredients

The following chart will give you some ideas about what substances act in what way in your hair. A magickal oil and herb chart for homemade beauty products can be found near the beginning of chapter 3. This list focuses only on the physical manifestations of various items. Consider adding them to any of the recipes in this chapter, depending upon your hair type.

Removes Sebum. Rosemary, jojoba, baking soda, witch hazel.

Breaks Up Oils. Rosemary, aloe vera, grapefruit, witch hazel, fennel.

Moisturizes. Almond oil, olive oil, banana flakes.

Stimulates Growth. Cedarwood oil.

Smoothes. Vitamin E oil, mint.

Takes Out Smells. Tomato juice, orange pulp.

Eases Dandruff. Tea tree oil.

Adds Shine, Brightens. Chamomile, hops, wine vinegar, catnip, hyssop.

Softens. Apple cider vinegar.

Thickens. Geranium, rosemary.

Dry Shampoo Base. Cornstarch.

For Blondes. Lemon, marigold, turmeric, yarrow, saffron, mullein.

For Redheads. Rosehips, red hibiscus, calendula, madder root.

For Brunettes. Sage, coffee, black walnut hulls (can stain skin and clothes!), cloves, black malva flowers, anise.

For Gray Hair. Potato peels, hollyhock, betony, yucca root.

Soap Agents. Castile soap, cream of tartar, sulfonated castor oil.

If you want to make the best magick, don't rush through the shampoo process as if you were late for work or school. Give yourself the time to fully appreciate the scent and feel of your magickal act, time to visualize and use words of power. You may want to light color-corresponding candles in the bathroom or have a mild incense burning. Take time to breathe in the aroma of the oils in the shampoo that are catalysts to your magick. These are actions that will trigger your deep mind that magick is afoot. Each time you engage in this ritualized action, your ability to work the spell will be that much stronger.

As with any spell, don't be a slave to the printed page. If you see components in one recipe you like and some more you like in others, experiment to find out if combining some of their best elements will work for you. You might want to look into Appendix B in the back of this book for a list of herbal side effects and interactions to avoid, but other than that your personal needs, affinities, and allergies should be the final arbiter of how your magickal shampoo is constructed, not this or any other spellbook.

The same is true for your words of power. If a spell doesn't have any, or doesn't have any you like, feel free to borrow them from other spells or to compose your own. Just take your time and make sure you're asking for what you really want and, preferably, that your words do not set up a situation where you are harming others or infringing upon their right of free will.

Remember that all the shampoo recipes given here are calibrated for a six to eight-ounce mixture. If you make more, your shampoo will be weaker, and if you make less, it may be too strong.

Shampoo to Attract New Love

2 drops lavender oil

1 drop rose oil

1 drop jasmine oil

1 drop neroli or orange oil

3 drops rosemary oil (only if your hair is oily)

6 drops almond oil (only if your hair is dry)

One last optional item for this spell is a lodestone or natural magnet. One can be empowered to attract new love into your life and placed at the bottom of your shampoo bottle to boost the spell's effectiveness.

Place the oils (or follow instructions for making a decoction) into a base of six ounces liquid castile soap. Because this recipe contains a soap product, it is a true shampoo that will cleanse as well as impart the magick you desire.

Be sure to envision your goal of finding a new love as you lather up your hair. Words of power might include:

continued . . .

Love who seeks me so world-weary,
Find me now, you who query;
I seek you now as you seek me,
Together forever, so mote it be.

Washing Away an Old Love

The popular stage musical *South Pacific* (1949) by Richard Rodgers (1901–1979) and Oscar Hammerstein II (1895–1960) presented us with an unforgettable scene in which a young nurse, played to legendary perfection by actress Mary Martin, washed her hair onstage every night to "wash that man right out" of her hair. For anyone unfamiliar with the scene, it was reprised by Mitzi Gaynor in a movie version that can be rented almost anywhere. The image is so magickal and so appropriate to the idea of psychic cleansing that it no doubt accounts for a large part of the memorability of the scene over more than a half-century later.

To wash a lover out of your life, combine the following.

4 ounces spring water

2 drops clove oil

¼ cup puréed pumpkin

¼ cup lime juice

1 tablespoon sulfonated castor oil

1 tablespoon liquid castile soap

Visualize your entire being—body, mind, and spirit—being freed of ties to the old love. Know that this part of your life is over and grounded as the soapy water spins down the drain. Emerge from the shower feeling free of the old ties and ready to start a new life for yourself. If you happen to know the lyrics to "I'm Gonna Wash That Man Right Outa My Hair" from *South Pacific*, then sing them loud and with feeling.

Banishing the Bad

A magickal shampoo can help you wash anything unwanted from your life. It can help you rid yourself a bad habit, bad job, bad acquaintances, bad situations, etc. To make these recipes adjust the shampoo in the previous recipe as follows.

To Break a Bad Habit. Add a pinch of ground yucca root or two drops juniper oil to help break the habitual urge.

To Leave a Bad Job. Add a single drop of myrrh oil to break the old job and two drops orange oil to help you attract a new one.

To Leave a Bad Situation. Add rainwater and birch bark powder for peace and a single drop of cinnamon for courage.

To Drop a Bad Friend. Add myrtle for love and good wishes, lemon verbena or lemon balm for comfort, and red clover for strength.

To Leave a Bad Home. Add rue for love and cedar for strength; add loosestrife to help you make the break from what is familiar.

Clear Thinking Shampoo

There are going to be times when you aren't sure what your magickal need is, or even if there is one. What you need is some privacy for thinking and something to help clear your thoughts so you can think. This shampoo and its heady scent will help you find that inner calm in which clarity of need can be discovered.

> 3 ounces spring water
>
> 2 ounces liquid castile soap
>
> 2 drops rosemary oil
>
> 2 drops angelica oil
>
> 2 drops bergamot oil
>
> 2 tablespoons apple cider vinegar
>
> ⅛ teaspoon baking soda

Fertility and Manifesting Shampoo

The egg is an eternal and universal symbol of rebirth. From its imagery may come not only traditional fertility magick, but all things manifested or birthed into the world. Keep in mind that eggs go bad very quickly, and this shampoo will not keep for more than a day if not refrigerated. In the refrigerator it will keep for about a week.

- 3 ounces spring water
- 2 ounces liquid castile soap
- 2 eggs whipped to a froth
- 3 drops olive or almond oil
- 1 drop allspice oil

An optional item is to add a moonstone to the bottom of the shampoo bottle to boost your magick with the fertile power of the mother moon.

Work it through your hair while visualizing what you want most manifesting in your life.

Beauty Shampoo

- 3 ounces spring water
- 2 ounces liquid castile soap
- 3 drops olive oil
- 2 drops violet oil
- 1 drop basil oil (add to incite passion)
- 3 tablespoon infusion of maidenhair

Those who see you will find you beautiful. You may wish to use this recipe in tandem with one of the glamoury spells in chapter 8.

Shampoo to Eliminate Obstacles

- 4 ounces spring water
- 1 ounce liquid castile soap
- 1 tablespoon chicory infusion

1 tablespoon thistle infusion

1 tablespoon fennel infusion

1 tablespoon anise infusion

1 tablespoon sulfonated castor oil

An optional item to add to this spell is a teaspoon of mistletoe infusion. It is good for boosting the spell but should never be ingested and should be kept far away from children and pets.

Mix all the ingredients. Seal the spell with words of power. The following quatrain is very generic and you should try to create another four lines that speaks directly to the obstacle you need removed from your path.

Locks that bind and doors that close,
Open to me, your secrets disclose;
That which is strewn to block by road,
You clear for me, your power I erode.

Curse Breaking Shampoo

One of the best uses of magickal soaps and shampoos is breaking curses. Even if you just feel you need to wash away the accumulation of negative psychic dirt, try this recipe.

½ cup wine vinegar

¼ cup lime juice

1 tablespoon comfrey decoction

1 drop peppermint oil

Blend in equal parts spring water and castile soap, about two ounces each.

By the powers both holy and profane,
I make your curse one placed in vain;
Your will cannot bind me, your curse is gone,
My will is supreme and my magick is strong.
Your efforts at harm I return to you,
To reap what you've sown is your destiny true;
Though I may not know your face or name,
For this harm only you now take the blame.

Lust and Passion Potion

    3 drops basil oil

    3 drops ginger oil

    2 tablespoons papaya juice

    2 teaspoons dill decoction

    1 teaspoon fenugreek decoction

Mix the ingredients in equal parts spring water and liquid castile soap, two to three ounces each. Wash your hair in this recipe to incite passion in your lover. Suggested words of power might be as follows.

Lover, this spell is my conveyance,
That you hold all others in abeyance;
I am the love that your passion ignites,
I am the passion your love incites.
To the thrill of passion we do subserve,
Anyone watching can our lust observe;
No other shall enter our circle of two,
Love and passion bind me to you.

Brain Boosting Shampoo

    ½ ounce liquid castile soap

    4 ounces spring water

    6 drops honeysuckle oil

    3 drops rosemary oil

    1 drop sage oil

    3 tablespoons sulfonated castor oil

Use this shampoo to give your powers of concentration a lift.

Purification Shampoo

2 ounces spring water

3½ ounces liquid castile soap

7 drops olive oil

3 drops acacia oil

2 tablespoons rose water or infusion

2 drops lotus oil (add before a lunar ritual)

2 drops nutmeg oil (add before a solar ritual)

2 drops sandalwood oil (add before an initiation rite)

Psychic Shampoo Blend

The precise blend of a psychic enhancer often depends on the psychic exercise you're seeking to enhance. The basic recipe given here will help open your psychic senses in general with suggestions for adding additional oils if you have a specific goal in mind for your psychic endeavors.

6 ounces liquid castile soap

6 drops sandalwood oil

3 drops myrrh oil

3 drops honeysuckle or acacia oil

1 drop juniper or pine oil

Optional Additions

2 drops marjoram (if contacting spirits)

2 drops lilac oil (if viewing past lives)

2 drops benzoin (to sense what's happening now)

2 drops jasmine oil (to have psychic dreams)

2 drops lavender or rose oil (for love divinations)

2 drops yarrow oil (to see the future)

Engage in your divination activity or other psychic exercise as soon as possible after using the shampoo.

To Keep You in Someone's Mind

1 ounce liquid castile soap

4 ounces spring water

3 drops cumin oil

3 drops lemon verbena oil

2 drops rosemary oil

1 drop juniper oil

2 tablespoons angelica infusion

1½ tablespoons sulfonated castor oil

Use while mentally projecting an image of your memory into the mind of someone not with you. Your words of power should contain some reference to a moment you shared with that person. Select a good memory to enhance the power of this spell. Suggested words of power of a generic nature follow, but please try to add a third quatrain to personalize this spell to your own history with the one in whose thoughts you wish to be. This imagery from your own memories are what will boost this spell the most.

> *To the sylphs* who rule the air I plea,*
> *Take to (name of person) good thoughts of me;*
> *With compassion be thee dutiful,*
> *Give (name of person) thoughts of me beautiful.*
>
> *Thoughts of me in his (or her) head dance,*
> *Thoughts of passion and romance;*
> *Faery-struck with daydreams be,*
> *(Name of person) thinks only of me.*

*Sylphs are the nature spirits who rule the element of air. Air is the element of communication and thought. In this spell you request that they carry thoughts of you to someone else. Sylphs are beings possessing free will and cannot be commanded. They should be thanked for their efforts when you finish your spell.

Peaceful Sleep and Dream Magick

    6 ounces spring water

    3 drops camphor oil

    3 drops lavender oil or gardenia oil

    3 drops jasmine oil (for psychic dreams)

    3 drops anise oil (for peace)

    1 tablespoon sulfonated castor oil

Lull yourself to sleep with thoughts of peaceful rest and, if your goal is prophetic dreams of the future, chant words of power to yourself as you fall asleep, such as:

> *By the power of three times three,*
> *I see the future as it shall be.*

Don't let that "as it shall be" line disturb you. All space and time exist in you and you have the power to make past and future what you will it to be. We have free will at all times to live our lives and we have the power of magick to help change our futures. If you see something you don't like coming at you head-on, then take steps now to alter that future, bending it to your will as any good Witch would. If all you want to do is see doom and gloom and then dwell on it and worry about it, what's the point in bothering to see the future at all? Remember the old adage, "Forewarned is forearmed."

Healing Shampoo

    6 ounces spring water

    3 drops angelica oil

    2 drops juniper oil

    1 drop cedar oil

    ¼ cup hyssop decoction

    1 tablespoon sulfonated castor oil

Use to support other healing efforts.

Shampoo to Find Needed Money

6 ounces liquid castile soap

3 drops pine oil

3 drops lemon oil

3 drops allspice oil

2 drops nutmeg oil

1 drop vetivert oil

An optional suggestion to is to place a silver or gold coin in the bottom of the shampoo bottle to enhance the spell's connection to that which we value as legal tender.

Use while visualizing your need for money. Be sure to back up your efforts in the physical world after the shampooing is done.

Being poor is really a bitch,
But magick alone will not make a rich Witch;
Yet prosperity comes with many faces,
My magickal will my poverty erases.

Dry Shampoo Spells

Dry shampoos have fallen from popularity since they were marketed with enthusiasm in the 1970s. They are not designed to replace regular shampoos but are to be an emergency stopgap when a full shampoo is not possible. They use absorbent powders to dry up oils that weigh down hair and make it appear dirty. They also absorb and mask odors from cooking fumes or cigarette smoke. Dry shampoos keep almost indefinitely when kept in sealed containers, but they do not have to be airtight. Their only drawback is that if your hair is really dirty it may take so much dry shampoo to make it appear clean that you take away its natural shine or cause it to look like your white, powdered head just popped out of the eighteenth century.

Fill a glass mixing bowl with about 10 ounces of cornstarch. Have a twelve-ounce jar to put the final product into. Add 1–2 teaspoons of finely powdered herbs to the mixture, depending on your magickal need:

Psychic Skills. Dill, marjoram, mugwort, thyme.

Attracting Love. Vervain, yarrow, myrtle, jasmine.

Inciting Lust. Fenugreek, basil, hyacinth, damiana.

Fertility. Bistort, hawthorn.

Fidelity. Sweet pea, thistle, chickweed, rye.

Money. Cowslip, comfrey, woodruff.

Curse Breaking. Vetivert, wintergreen, galangal.

Healing. Fennel, bay, feverfew, boneset.

Mental Prowess. Rosemary, sage.

Protection. Cinnamon, clove, bay, nutmeg.

Brush a small portion through your hair to clean, working carefully around the roots so you don't leave a buildup of white powder that looks like dandruff or some kind of skin disease. Do this while visualizing your goal. Fluff out your hair, check once more for white residue, and seal the spell with any words of power you have chosen.

Magickal Hair Conditioners

Hair is made up of protein layers composed of dead skin cells. Nonliving cells can never be healed, they may only be cosmetically enhanced. This is why, as was mentioned when discussing skin care products, there is no hair product that can truly repair damaged hair. Once the harm is done, it's done. You can improve the appearance and texture of hair by using products that help close and smooth the cuticle to give the temporary appearance of repair, but the next day the effect is gone and the treatment will need to be repeated.

Many conditioners on the market hype themselves as rich in proteins or botanicals that are able to repair hair, but it's simply not true. The advertisers get away with these exaggerations—in the United States, at least—because the

Food and Drug Administration can't keep up with the backlog of products whose claims they must investigate for fraudulence or tighter regulation.

Even among users of all-natural hair conditioners, protein products are hyped as repair tool. The sad fact is that popular proteins like eggs and nut oils probably do not have molecules small enough to penetrate the hair shaft and therefore strengthen it. Most of the proteins that are small enough to penetrate are chemically engineered and are included in expensive salon conditioners. These sounds like a good thing at first, but they are still not proven to permanently fix anything except higher profit margins for the cosmetic companies.

Does this mean we shouldn't use any of these products or keep working with proteins? Of course not. The very word "cosmetic" means to put on a facade or provide an appearance that belies what's underneath the surface. Anything that makes us think we look better—which will consequently make us feel better—is worth a try, and many of these popular conditioning products do wonders for the outward appearance of our hair. They do this primarily by smoothing the cuticle and plumping up the shaft to give the illusion of softness and fullness.

As with magickal shampoos, magickal hair conditioners can be concocted for any magickal need. They can be used alone after a standard shampooing or in tandem with a magickal shampoo. You may add any of the oils or ingredients to your homemade conditioners discussed in the section on magickal shampoos, with the exceptions of castile soap or sulfonated castor oil, which are soap agents. It's also best to avoid astringents such as rosemary that tend to strip natural oils rather than soften and smooth.

Just as was in the case of your homemade shampoos, you are probably not going to be using preservatives in your homemade conditioners. With conditioners you are also using substances that are even more likely to go bad much faster than you would expect. Make no more than six ounces of your magickal conditioner at a time and store it in a tightly capped jar in a cool dry place such as the refrigerator.

Mayonnaise and Egg for Manifestation

This conditioner will not only improve the appearance of your hair but provide fertile ground for manifesting your wishes or enhancing your fertility. Remember that eggs do not keep for long. This conditioner will stay fresh in the refrigerator for only about a week.

> 6 eggs whipped to a froth
>
> ½ cup real mayonnaise (not salad dressing)

Whip the mixture together with an egg beater or electric mixer; just be sure to keep your end goal visualization clear as you mix. Work the mixture well into your hair, leave for three to five minutes, and rinse.

A desire in me has been awakened,
A need that shall not be forsaken;
By all the magick that I do best,
My desire in this world does manifest.

Love Attracting Conditioner

> ⅓ cup puréed avocado
>
> 2 tablespoons raw honey
>
> 2 teaspoons wheat germ oil
>
> 2 teaspoons apricot kernel oil
>
> 2 drops violet oil

This recipe makes enough for one conditioning treatment. Work it well into your hair while visualizing love being drawn your way. Leave on for five minutes, then rinse. Suggested words of power follow.

Love that's new and fresh and free,
Unknown lover, come to me;
Romance, passion, feels so right,
I draw my true love to me this night.

Hair Softening Conditioner to Enhance Beauty

½ cup apple cider vinegar

1 teaspoon wheat germ oil

1 teaspoon ginseng or maidenhair decoction

3 drops tea tree oil

Mix well into your hair while envisioning your beauty radiating to everyone who sees you. Visualize the shine and softness of your hair like a halo that makes you stand out in a crowd. This spell can be used in tandem with the glamoury spells in chapter 8 or coupled with any other love attracting spell to boosts its effectiveness.

Use these words of power to quell any appearance competition from others and to make yourself the most eye-catching vision in the place.

With this spell I do dispatch,
Any other person who an eye might catch;
I'm the most intriguing, anyone can see,
I draw every eye to the beauty that is me.
No other person can hope to compete,
With my appearance to any they meet;
I sparkle and shine and all others fade,
My reputation as wonderful is now made.

Hot Oil Treatment for Any Need

Hot oil treatments are popular hair care products that improve the looks of split ends and enhance shine. With this recipe you have the option of adding a single drop of any other oil so that you can make the hot oil treatment work as a magickal catalyst for any need. Look to the charts and suggestions for shampoo oils to glean ideas.

This basic recipe will not only improve the look of your hair, but increase your personal magickal power. Omit the ylang ylang oil when making hot oil treatments for other types of magick, and add a drop of the nonirritating oil that best corresponds to your need. This recipe is enough for one treatment of average-length hair.

¼ ounce apricot kernel oil

¼ ounce olive oil

1 drop ylang ylang

Heat the oil by placing it in a thin plastic container and then placing the container into a pan of very hot tap water. It's best not to try and heat the oil on the stove top or in a microwave or it could become dangerously hot or even catch fire. You want the oil to be very warm, but not so warm it burns. If the oil is warm but still comfortable to your touch, then it's ready to use. Work the oil into hair and scalp, then wrap in a warm towel. Keep hair covered for ten minutes, then rinse.

six

Perfumes and Aromatherapy

Give me beauty in the inward soul;
And may the outward and inward . . . be at one.
—Plato

Our sense of smell is a primitive thing. It can conjure up a thought, evoke an emotion, bring back a memory, aid concentration, or change our mood. It can attract lovers, create atmosphere, repel pests or negative influences, mask unpleasant odors, soothe the spirit, or make us fit for being in the presence of deity.

Magickal perfumery is an art almost inseparable from the pseudoscience of aromatherapy. Aromatherapy is the belief that certain scents trigger specific emotional or physiological responses in people simply because specific natural odors evoke them, not because the substance has been magickally empowered. To the contrary, many practitioners of aromatherapy, including a growing number of physicians, would scoff at magick as being any more than delusion. This is why I refer to it as a pseudoscience.

Magickal practitioners know that if an aromatic substance, for example, evokes romantic feelings in someone, then it is probable it is a substance that has been used in love spells for hundreds of years and that magickally empowering it to its task will only enhance its performance. This is one of the primary distinctions of the two arts. Aromatherapists believe that a potion has to smell pleasing to be successful. Magickal practitioners know that, on occasion, it is the least-pleasant smelling substances that work the best. Aromatherapists only concern themselves with the effects of smell. Magickal practitioners concern themselves with the energy in the plant from which the smell was derived. The fact that individual skin chemistry affects the scent of oils should not be an issue in magickal perfumery unless you're attempting to concoct a purely cosmetic blend. Please keep this distinction in mind when working with perfumery. Magicians may decide to add aromatherapies to their art to enhance it, but it is rare that an aromatherapist will add magick, either from lack of acceptance or from its incompatibility in a specific scent formula.

Create your magickal perfumes according to the same instructions given for making oil blends in chapter 2. Your creation of them should not be rushed. They should be blended with care in a half-ounce or more of base oil.

It is even more essential to allow your scent to "marry" in magickal perfumery than in almost any other kind of oil magick. Scent should be a key player in this art; much less so than the energy of the plants, but much more so than in any other type of herbal magick. The professional perfumer knows that not all scents are created equal. Not only are some stronger and others more subtle, but some evaporate more quickly. These are usually the ones we notice most when we first use a perfume. Professionals refer to this as the top note. After thirty minutes or so we smell another scent dominating: the middle note. After another couple hours we smell the scent that evaporates the least quickly, the subtle after-fragrance known to perfumers as the bottom note.

All the notes are altered by their having been married to one another, but one always dominates. This is what causes the top, middle, and bottom notes to come out in turn. Be aware that the oil with the strongest scent may not end up being the bottom note. It may be the top note, evaporate, and leave the other scents to dominate. This unpredictability of scent is what makes perfumery a true art.

Another factor affecting the development of scent is the process by which the oil has been extracted from its plant source, though it is impossible to know from the label on a product which method was used. Often times you will find that one company's 100 percent pure oil smells better to you than another's. This is likely due to a difference in processing methods.

Sometimes perfumers find only one method that works on a particular plant, other times they may choose the one they prefer. The four methods are expression, extraction, enfleurage, and maceration. Expression is the least reliable. It uses high heat to get the oils, and often they must be clarified by other processes or blended with other oils to approximate the desired scent. The result may be all natural but not all pure. Extraction uses solvents rather than heat, similar to making a tincture. In enfleurage the plant is soaked in fats to break down the oils. Maceration uses both fats and heat.

You should never place undiluted essential oils directly on your skin. Even when they are diluted you should use caution. Take care to note any substances to which you are allergic, or which may irritate your skin or cause a photosynthetic reaction if you are out in the sun. Citrus oils are infamous for causing these rashes.

Use only natural essential oils in magickal perfumes. Avoid using any product labeled a perfumed oil. These are synthetics that will not give you the truest scent and will not blend well with other oils. These can sometimes work in a pinch for aromatherapy but they are void of magickal energy.

Keep your oils away from fabric. Oils stain badly and irrevocably. You may want to consider placing a small bit of oil on a cotton ball and concealing it on your person rather than risking the oil coming into contact with your clothing or skin.

Another suggestion to try if you dilute and dilute and still feel your magickal perfumes are too strong or too irritating is to make a decoction first and add this to a base oil instead. Chapter 1 will give you instructions for making these. The resulting scent will be subtle in the extreme but just as potent for magick.

Perfume blends made with decoctions will need to be shaken well each time you use them since the oil perfume base and the water-based decoction will tend to separate.

Using a decoction in your magickal perfume is a good method for adding the energy of a plant for which you have the herb readily available but not the essential oil. It is also a way to add the energy of an herb for which an oil is not available, such as saffron, which is costly and has not been available commercially for years.

Keep in mind that some oils are hard to process or else produce so little oil per pound of plant that their cost is outrageous. Tuberose is one example. In cases such as these the dried plants are easier to come by and much less expensive. If you want the essence of such herbs in your magickal perfumes consider using decoctions for these too.

Oils that have very strong odors, such as angelica and patchouly, should be used sparingly. These strong scents are often bottom-note fragrances whose scents linger long after the rest of the essences have evaporated. To save money, buy smaller vials of these strongly scented oils. You won't need to use as much of them and you don't want them to go rancid on you.

You should empower your oil blends once they are complete by presenting the bottle to the light of the moon or the sun and reciting words of power that strengthen your visualization of the oil's goal. Wear the oil when you want to draw to you the thing you created it to attract. Some suggested words of power follow many of the spells in the next section. If you create your own words of power for a spell, carefully read through them to be sure you've asked for exactly what you want.

Magickal Perfumes

The perfume recipes that follow are not the only combinations that will help you achieve your end goals. Note also that if the scent of a magickal perfume is too overwhelming for you, you can place most of these oils in a lotion or soap base (see chapters 3 and 4) in which they will be more diluted. Their magick will be just as potent but their scent and the possibility of side effects will be lessened.

Romantic Attraction Perfume

6 drops jasmine

6 drops vanilla

2 drops lavender

2 drops rose

As you place this feminine, floral scent on you, you may want to use words of power, ones you can repeat to yourself when you meet someone whose interest you want to attract. This works best in an olive oil base.

Lavender purple and roses red,
Now my face shall dance in his head;
Jasmine yellow and vanilla of gold,
His attraction to me is strong and bold.

Enhancing Beauty #1

8 drops apricot

4 drops linden blossom

3 drops geranium

This oil blend is great to wear when doing one of the glamoury spells in chapter 8. Their energies are very sympathetic and the perfume can help your chosen glamoury trigger work to greater effect.

Enhancing Beauty #2

6 drops white hyacinth

4 drops apple blossom

3 drops sweet pea

Use as described in the previous perfume recipe to project an image of beauty. This works best in an apricot kernal oil base.

To Boost Personal Energy

5 drops basil

3 drops cypress

2 drops ginger

1 drop spearmint

Wear or sniff when you need a boost of vigor.

Brain Boosting Perfume

5 drops oakmoss

4 drops sage

3 drops rosemary

2 drops marjoram or benzoin

Wear or sniff before studying or taking an exam. I recommend you use your words of power three times while using this perfume: one, when putting the oil on; two, just before you start to study or take a test; and three, during a study session or exam if possible.

Energy of the brain I call,
Help me absorb and help me recall;
Power of thought and intellect be,
Ever strong and able in me.

Astral Projection Perfume

9 drops parsley

6 drops mugwort

1 drop angelica

Use before attempting astral projection.

Open shall be the world unseen,
Admit me now as a spirit being;
I travel in safety as warded I be,
The astral world now opens to me.

Fertility Perfume

9 drops avocado

3 drops carrot seed

2 drops hazel

Use while doing fertility spells to boost their power or place on chakra points prior to having sex if your goal is getting pregnant. The magick of this blend works best in an almond oil base. Avoid using almond oil if you are allergic to nuts; substitute olive oil instead.

Otherworld Contact Perfume

3 drops lavender

1 drop angelica

½ drop cinnamon

You may wear this blend if the cinnamon does not irritate your skin, or you may use it to anoint candles when attempting to contact spirits or open the doors to the otherworld.

Deities, spirits, and faeries of old,
Our meeting in the otherworld has been foretold;
I humbly seek admittance to this glorious place,
As I prove myself worthy of entering this space.
I come as a seeker and know I must pass,
The threshold terrors that block my path;
With courage and knowledge I welcome this test,
So my spiritual life may be at its best.

Love Perfume #1

3 drops vanilla

3 drops myrtle

1 teaspoon tincture of rue

continued . . .

Use this subtle scent as a love attracting magickal perfume or as an aid to any other love spell. This oil makes an effective anointing oil for candles used in love magick. Empower the oil with your goal through words of power.

Love, yet elusive, breaks down my door,
Storms into my life leaving me wanting no more;
Fulfilling and rapturous, romantic and kind,
The love I seek does me now find.

Love Perfume #2

6 drops violet

4 drops orange or bergamot

2 drops rose

2 drops hyacinth

Use to attract or enhance romantic love, as described in the previous perfume recipe.

To Attract a Woman's Romantic Interest

6 drops nutmeg

3 drops orange

3 drops clove

1 drop bay

1 drop witch hazel

1 drop vanilla

Wear this blend or use it as a candle-anointing oil to attract the romantic attention of women. Try a base of safflower oil.

For Finding Employment

2 drops pine

2 drops juniper

2 drops clove

Use during your job-seeking period or before job interviews. This perfume can also be used to anoint candles in spells to help you find employment.

To Obtain Needed Money

6 drops honeysuckle

4 drops vervain

2 drops dill

2 drops magnolia

Wear during spells to obtain money and prosperity, or use as a candle-anointing oil during spells for wealth.

> *What I seek is no more than I need,*
> *Magickal perfume, now do the deed;*
> *I get the cash without any ruse,*
> *I ask only for what I need to use.*

For Boosting Moon Magick

5 drops narcissus

5 drops sandalwood

3 drops lotus

3 drops myrrh

1 drop lemon

Wear during esbat rituals and when working magick attuned to the lunar cycles.

> *Lady Luna, I ask your blessing,*
> *As I work spells to you addressing;*
> *All my love and will I give,*
> *Bless this magick that it does live.*

Healing Perfume

6 drops carnation

3 drops geranium

3 drops rosemary

1 drop coriander

Wear or sniff to assist in healing—both magickal healing and that prescribed by a physician. If you are sick, do not be tempted to use magick alone. Magickal healing works best in tandem with modern medicine. With a little effort you can find a doctor sympathetic to your interest in alternative healing methods as a support for standard medical treatment.

For Inner Peace and Harmony

4 drops vanilla

4 drops bergamot

4 drops sandalwood

Wear or sniff this perfume when you need to seek inner peace or create harmony in your surroundings.

Peace and harmony, act as a balm,
Give to me a sense of calm;
Stress is busted, anxieties flee,
Serenity now shines forth from me.

Protection Perfume #1

4 drops frankincense

3 drops black pepper

3 drops spearmint

Protection needs can be psychic or physical or a combination of both. Remember again that magick works best with commonsense efforts to back up your spell. Don't do things or go places where you are in danger and expect magick alone to protect you. Try this in a coconut oil base.

My mind and body I do ward,
Protection from the mob and horde;
No spirit or person of baneful sway,
May harm me now in any way.

Protection Perfume #2

7 drops basil

3 drops copal

Use as described in the previous perfume spell to evoke protective energy.

To Bring Out Your Vivacity

4 drops ginger

2 drops palm

2 drops bay

1 drop yarrow

Sport this scent when you wish to project a vital, energetic image.

Consolation Perfume

6 drops marigold

4 drops lemongrass

3 drops linden blossoms

Wear or sniff to attain consolation or to help relieve grief.

Dream Magick Perfume

4 drops jasmine

2 drops bergamot

2 drops lotus

2 drops lilac (add for past life dreams)

Wear or sniff to induce prophetic dreams. You can also make a little magick pillow out of these same herbs and place it under your regular pillow to further strengthen your dream magick spell.

To Bring Out Passion and Lust

4 drops cardamom

4 drops ylang ylang

½ drop patchouly

Wear or use as a candle-anointing oil to bring out the passion in your romantic partner.

Passion's fire, gold and bright,
Inflame my love's desire tonight;
Lusting, longing, wanting me,
Our passion and love shall always be.

Psychic Enhancement Perfume

3 drops yarrow

3 drops mimosa

3 drops laurel

Wear before performing divinations or to heighten your psychic senses.

Get Noticed Perfume

3 drops vetivert

3 drops vanilla

1 drop anise

Wear to make yourself stand out in a crowd.

Perfume for Purification Rituals

5 drops cypress

5 drops sandalwood

3 drops wisteria

2 drops cedarwood

2 drops tea tree

Wear during purification rites. You may also add this oil to soaps or lotions whose magickal goal is purification (see chapters 3 and 4).

The Scents

Because of the subjective nature of scent, you will need to experiment with blends that both smell good to you and work magickally and aromatically to achieve your goals. Just as you do not always like the same perfume as your best friend, you are not going to work as well with the same magickal perfume blends as anyone else. Within the framework of your magickal goals, there should be hundreds of ways to create perfume spells to suit yourself.

The following is a general list of aromatic oils that fall into the categories of either top, middle, or bottom notes. Keep in mind that the amount of each scent you use in proportion to others, and the length of time you allow the scents to marry before using them, will affect the way they develop once they are mixed with your unique skin chemistry.

Top Notes. Bergamot, black pepper, carnation, cedar, cedarwood, chamomile, coriander, cumin, eucalyptus, fennel, jasmine, lavender, lemon, lotus, myrrh, pine, rose, sage, sweet pea, violet, wintergreen, wormwood.

Middle Notes. Acacia, allspice, animal oils, cardamom, cinnamon, clary sage, clove, copal, geranium, hyacinth, lemon verbena, lilac, nutmeg, oakmoss, orris root, peppermint, rosemary, tuberose, ylang ylang.

Bottom Notes. Angelica, benzoin, camphor, clover, cypress, galangal, gardenia, ginger, ginseng, hyacinth, juniper, magnolia, neroli, patchouly, sandalwood, vanilla.

Perfumers enjoy experimenting with scents that are reputed to not marry well to find new ways to blend old favorites. Individual scents fall roughly into categories, some of which are thought to work well together and others which are thought otherwise. Be aware, as always, that personal tastes vary on these point. The categories are:

Woods and Grasses

Citrus

Florals

Orientals and Spices

Herbals

Fruits

Animal Oils and Musks

Fixatives

Fixatives may add scent to the blend, but their primary function is to retard evaporation of the top note and help hold the scent in place once it has married to the perfumer's satisfaction.

This chapter concludes with a brief list of oils that have specific aromatic or magickal properties. This list covers common uses and may not apply 100 percent to you. Don't be afraid to color outside the lines and try something new that just may be the greatest magickal success you've ever created. Occult supply shops carry or can get you almost as many oils as there are plants. Your choices really are limitless.

Scents that Calm and Soothe. Bayberry, bergamot, chamomile, eucalyptus, jasmine, lotus, narcissus, sandalwood.

Scents that Uplift and Stimulate. Basil, clove, cypress, nutmeg, orange, peppermint, pine, tea tree.

Scents that Help Balance Emotions. Carnation, cedar, copal, lavender, linden blossom, patchouly, rosemary, wintergreen.

Scents that Attract Men. Almond, jasmine, lavender, musk, sandalwood, vanilla.

Scents that Attract Women. Allspice, apricot, bayberry, juniper, lime, mastic, mimosa, moss, orange, sandalwood.

For Spells for Love and Romance. Galangal, jasmine, lavender, lemon verbena, lotus, marjoram, melissa, mimosa, myrtle, orange blossom, orris root, palmarosa, rose, rue, tuberose, vervain, vetivert, yarrow.

For Spells for Healing. Angelica, calendula, carnation, coriander, fennel, galangal, peppermint, pine, rosemary, willow, witch hazel.

For Spells for Fidelity. Comfrey, cumin, galangal, magnolia, spearmint, yucca.

For Spells for Beauty. Apple blossom, apricot, honeysuckle, jonquil, lavender, narcissus, sweet pea, tuberose, violet, white hyacinth.

For Spells for Money or Employment. Allspice, aloe, bergamot, clove, dill, fenugreek, ginger, heather, honeysuckle, juniper, moss, pine, tarragon, vervain.

For Spells for Fertility. Almond, avocado, carrot seed, hazel, lemongrass, palm, peach, pear, pine.

For Spells for Lust and Passion. Cardamom, clove, galangal, marjoram, nutmeg, hibiscus, papaya, rosemary, rue.

For Spells for Courage and Stamina. Bay, benzoin, cardamom, cedarwood, columbine, galangal, juniper, rosemary.

For Spells for Protection. Basil, bay, birch, black pepper, clove, cinnamon, copal, frankincense, lime, nutmeg, orange, wisteria.

For Spells for Psychic Exercises. Angelica, elder, galangal, gardenia, jasmine, lemongrass, laurel, lilac, lily, marigold, melissa, myrrh, yarrow.

For Spells for Purification. Acacia, anise, birch, coconut, fennel, frankincense, hyssop, olive, sandalwood.

Magick with oils and scents has always been very popular, and now aromatherapy has enjoyed an explosion of interest in popular culture. There are several books on magickal oil use which you may find interesting if you want to pursue this art in depth: Scott Cunningham's *Magical Herbalism* (Llewellyn, 1982) and *The Complete Book of Incense, Oils and Brews* (Llewellyn, 1989), Richard Alan Miller and Iona Miller's *The Magical and Ritual Use of Perfumes* (Destiny, 1990), and Anna Riva's *Golden Secrets of Mystic Oils* (self-published, 1990). The Millers' book is one of my personal favorites because of their emphasis on Kaballistic correspondences and their interesting breakdowns of scent styles.

Anna Riva commercially packages and sells blended oils for a variety of needs. They smell nice and have a good reputation for effectiveness if you empower them. I've always been fond of her Bewitching Oil for use in love spells. Her oil blends can be found or ordered through most any occult shop (see Appendix A for mail order and web resources).

I won't attempt to list all the books currently available on aromatherapy as it would be a volume in itself, but I did recently come across one that contained literally hundreds of interesting nonmagickal formularies titled *500 Formulas for Aromatherapy* by David Schiller and Carol Schiller (Sterling Publications, 1994). Scott Cunningham also wrote a book combining magick and aromatherapy called *Magical Aromatherapy: The Power of Scent* (Llewellyn, 1989), which can help spur your creative imagination. Also look in the health and beauty sections of your library or bookstore for other titles of interest.

seven
Ritual and
Magickal Makeup

Goddess to thy shrine we come,
Thy sweet magic brings us together.
—Fredrich von Schiller

Feminists argue that the colorful makeup plastering the faces of today's women is no more than a mimicry of sexual arousal designed to reinforce the concept that women are all evil temptresses who deserve a lesser roll in society—and less of that society's privilege and wealth. It's sometimes hard to find fault with this argument, or to deny the obvious power the makeup and fashion industry has over women (this argument is detailed in *The Beauty Myth: How Images of Beauty Are Used Against Women* by Naomi Wolf [Anchor, 1992]; I recommend it if you enjoy a well-structured bashing of big business).

Certainly the choice to use facial cosmetics or not should be an individual's right, and this book deliberately avoids taking either side in this emotionally charged

145

issue. Many women who practice magick, especially those involved in Pagan religions, use cosmetics as ritual enhancement, which was one of the original functions of makeup.

Like masking, makeup allowed the woman to take on the persona of a deity, elemental, or spirit during spells and ritual. Hollywood makeup artists still make these transformations of ordinary human beings into extraordinary creatures on a daily basis. Aside from the fantastic beings we imagine them to be when we suspend our willingness of disbelief—itself a magickal state of consciousness—we also see Sir Lawrence Olivier made up as an African man to play Othello and Eddie Murphy fooling the eye as a Euro-American. These tricks of the eye using makeup do not fall into the offensive category of "black face" that Euro-American actors adopted during the late nineteenth and early twentieth centuries, but are professional stage makeup illusions in which the actor best suited for the part is used as the base for the illusion the makeup artist seeks to create.

Hollywood makeup maven Kevin Acoin's lavishly illustrated book *Face Forward* (Little, Brown & Co., 2000) shows how he achieves these dramatic transformations with today's most popular actors. The book is well worth a look if you are attracted to the idea of using makeup as masking in a ritual setting. It can give you lots of great ideas and stimulate your creative imagination.

Using makeup to enhance personal appearance or to denote rank in society probably dates further back into prehistory than any of us can imagine. Extant illustrations from Egypt more than 4,500 years old depict faces richly enhanced with makeup. These faces include those of servants, slaves, and men, as well as the famous historical beauty Queen Cleopatra (69–30 B.C.E.). In the late eighteenth century, upper-class men in North America and Europe sported lip and cheek rouge, arguably yet another mimicry of sexual arousal. Makeup for Western men fell from favor after the early nineteenth century, an era when women who attempted to use makeup for cosmetic enhancement were eschewed as sexually loose.

This chapter has three sections: spells using popular cosmetics; a ritual of Venus designed to enhance personal beauty, however you view it; and a ritual designed to attune the practitioner to the great mother Goddess Isis, Egypt's queen of heaven and earth. If using makeup in any form offends you, please skip this chapter or find ways to adapt these spells and rituals that suits your worldview. Neither way is inherently right or wrong.

Spells Using Everyday Makeup

The spells in this section use commercially prepared cosmetics as their catalysts. The selection of type, brand, and color is yours to make. It is best to purchase new cosmetics when you will be using them as magickal tool. It is best not to try to empower an old cosmetic that you've already used for mundane purposes to work as a catalyst for magick. Just as you would not use the same unempowered candle you sought out during a power outage for magick, you do not want to use the same cosmetics that have not previously served magickal functions for use in your bath and beauty spells.

It may surprise you to find that this section will not try to convince you to make your own cosmetics out of plant or vegetable dyes. I've tried hundreds of these, and they have some serious drawbacks. The kohl used as eyeliner and shadow in centuries past causes infection and blindness, and the beet and berry juices used for lip and cheek color are hard to place with accuracy and they cause serious staining. As long as there are so many longer-lasting, safer, and easier to apply options to be found at your local drugstore, it just makes sense to use them. (If you find yourself craving a berry juice blush, you might want to look into *Herbal Body Book* by Jeanne Rose [Frog Ltd., 2000], which has a chapter on making plant-based cosmetics.)

The same is true for makeup removers. Most women know that it is skin-smart to remove all traces of makeup at least once a day to avoid clogged pores and breakouts. "Natural" makeup enthusiasts recommend heavy oils like baby oil, olive oil, mineral oil, petroleum jelly, or castor oil to remove the daily buildup, especially around the delicate eye area. The drawback to any oil-based makeup remover is that it can clog your pores worse than any commercial cosmetic (meaning it is a comedogenic) and will cause your eyes to be swollen and puffy the next morning (meaning it's ugly). Another drawback is that if you're taking off your eye makeup to start over fresh, oily removers will cling to lashes and skin until they wear off naturally and will prevent fresh cosmetics from adhering. Plain soap and water or commercially prepared, nonoily makeup removers have always been, and still are, your cleanest choices for thorough and easy makeup removal.

The Irresistible Kiss Enchantment

For this spell you will need only a new tube of lipstick and a single drop of lemon oil. Rub the lemon oil lightly and sparingly over the shaft of the lipstick, being careful not to break it off from the tube. Be sure to visualize the oil and the lipstick coming together with magickal potency to create a substance that will make your lips irresistibly kissable.

As you apply the lipstick, think of yourself as the world's most devastating femme fatale. Know that your lips will be watched with dreamy anticipation. Seal your spell with words of power.

> *Lips so full and soft and fair,*
> *Kiss me, kiss me, if you dare;*
> *He has no doubt it will be such bliss,*
> *He has no doubt I crave his kiss.*

The Keep-Him-Guessing Enchantment

If you'd rather play games than be kissed, you can keep your target guessing "does she want to kiss me or not" by taking the above spell and substituting lemongrass or primrose oil for the lemon oil. Empower the lipstick to give your lips qualities of playfulness and capriciousness instead of willing compliance. Think of yourself as emulating the capricious attitude of the fey, or faery folk, rather than that of a femme fatale.

> *As insouciant as springtime,*
> *As capricious as the fey;*
> *Shall I? Will I? Tomorrow or today?*
> *With laughter bright as sunshine,*
> *And lips as soft as night,*
> *Maybe . . . maybe . . . you shall kiss me tonight.*

Eyes of Truth Spell

Instead of merely sizing up someone's body language to assess whether you are being told truths or lies, take some magickal steps that will make it much harder for someone to look you in the eyes and tell you falsehoods. To do this you need only some eye makeup. If you use anything with a blue cast to it, all the better. Blue is the color of fidelity and truth: Think "true blue." Just don't wear something that doesn't look good on you for the sake of adding the color element.

As you line your eyes, brush on mascara, or add contour and shadow, visualize those from whom you want the truth gazing into your eyes during normal conversation. See your eyes mesmerizing the speaker, drawing from him or her the essence of truthfulness. As long as that person is face to face with you, lying will be difficult, if not impossible.

When you are done making up your eyes, gaze into your reflection and seal the spell with words of power.

With truth and faith these eyes do shine,
No lie passes these eyes of mine;
With each blink and with each stare,
The truth alone shall be laid bare.

More Eye Magick

Raw potatoes or cucumber slices placed over closed eyes reduces puffiness and is also soothing and relaxing. You may wish to consider ending your day with this type of beauty treatment after you have removed your makeup. A relaxed face and a good night's rest are two of the best appearance enhancers known. You can also magickally empower the potato to help ground and center you, and the cucumber to enhance beauty and attract wealth.

The Beauty Spot

Beauty spots have come and gone in popularity for hundreds of years. The idea that someone could take what most people would perceive as a flaw or blemish on the skin and turn it into a trademark beauty asset is really magick. Think of Cindy Crawford's famous mole or the beauty spot sported by Elizabeth Taylor in *Cat on a Hot Tin Roof.* The Hollywood spin doctors did a great job turning two classic beauties and one supposed flaw into an emblem of beauty sought out by other women.

Blemishes that attract the opposite sex are hallmarks of many love stories in myth and folk legends. One of the most famous belonged to a man, Diarmuid of the Love Spot, in Irish mythology. He kept his hair combed down over the flaw on his forehead knowing that if women viewed it, they would fall immediately in love with him. Beauty spots can be created with eye pencils and empowered as amulets that attract the romantic attention of the opposite sex.

The Speech Guardian Spell

If you have to make a speech and are worried about tripping over your own tongue, or if you just want to avoid "foot in mouth disease" in saying something you fear you'll regret, empower any new tube of lipstick as a word guardian. Imbue it with the energy to help you speak so that you will be understood and will not say anything that later makes you feel awkward or embarrassed. Seal the spell with words of power each time you put the lipstick on.

> *Circle round the lips does reach,*
> *Guard my tongue and watch my speech;*
> *Each word considered with thought I take,*
> *Sounds of indiscretion I do not make.*

Radiant Self-Confidence

Blushing cheeks were once considered a sign of being shy or demur. Now we associate ruddy cheeks with sparkling good health and self-confidence. To be viewed as healthy and capable, place your blusher on your cheeks while chanting words of power.

> *Radiant health and confidence shines,*
> *Illuminate this face of mine;*
> *Bold and sassy, brave and smart,*
> *I inspire faith while winning the heart.*

Assisting Invisibility

The art of becoming invisible was one of the magickal tricks that most concerned and fascinated the Witch hunters of the Middle Ages, but it really isn't all that mysterious. Usually it refers to the art of astral projection, or sending the consciousness out to view other places and times. It can also refer to mentally pulling yourself into the background, or out of sight.

It is this last technique of invisibility that makeup can best help you achieve. If you want to recede into the background or go unnoticed, empower your makeup foundation or concealer as an aid to helping you remain invisible. As you apply it, recite your words of power again and again as you visualize yourself becoming less dense; fading, becoming harder to see in your everyday world.

> *Into the background I now fade,*
> *Fully transparent I must be made;*
> *Unnoticed, unseen, by eyes that probe,*
> *I move about cloaked in an astral robe.*

Be sure to reverse the spell when you're ready to be noticed again or when it would be dangerous not to be easily seen, such as while you're driving. Visualize yourself growing more dense and easy to see in your everyday world as you reverse your words of power.

> *I make the change from spirit to form,*
> *From an empty cold spot to a body warm;*
> *I'm solid and vibrant, a presence clear,*
> *This cannot be mistaken, I simply am here.*

Hiding the Emotions Spell

We all know that it's not good to bottle our emotions up inside, but sometimes the demands of life require that we find that proverbial stiff upper lip and carry on until wallowing in our anguish is appropriate. Use a powder compact to help get you through your day without those crazy feelings inside spilling out. As you press the powder onto your face, visualize your inner turmoils being patted down, buried, and invisible under the face your must present to the world.

> *Pat down the feeling, pat down the woes;*
> *No one sees the turmoil, neither friends nor foes;*
> *Pleasant and in control I seem to all I see,*
> *Pat down the feelings until alone I can be.*

Holding in the Lip Magick

Seal any ongoing lipstick spell by adding neutral lip liner as the final touch. As you encircle your lips with the liner, visualize that it is surrounding and containing that which you have worked hard to attain. For example, if you've worked hard on a spell to get your intended lover to kiss you, make sure your lip liner holds his interest after that first kiss is won.

The Beauty of Venus

The Roman Goddess Venus—or her Greek counterpart Aphrodite—is known the world over as a Goddess of love and beauty thanks to Italian painter Sandro Bottocelli's *The Birth of Venus* (1458). Hanging today in the Galleria degli Uffizi in Florence, it depicts Venus, born in the full flower of young womanhood, arising from the heart of a clam shell at the edge of a mythic sea. A light breeze wraps her long, pale hair around her voluptuousness, which she modestly attempts to conceal. In the fifteenth century she was as much the beauty image to strive for as any fashion model is today.

That this Goddess was beautiful and desirable beyond the normal standards of attraction is noted with excessive hyperbole in the writings of Greek poet Homer (circa eighth century B.C.E.), who composed at least two hymns to her honor. One of these contains the effusive lines, "I will sing of stately Aphrodite, gold-crowned and beautiful. . . . who stirs up sweet passions [in the] Gods and and mortal man, and all the birds that fly through the air and the many creatures of the earth."

Aphrodite's Roman counterpart, Venus, shares her attributes and is often evoked to assist with spells for love and beauty. The planet that is named for her is associated with her color, green, and green is magickally associated with the attainment of a more desirable personal appearance.

The Venusian Beauty Ritual

For this ritual you will need a small mirror, one big enough to see no more than your neck and face. You will need a green powder, such as an eye shadow or color-correcting face powder compact. You will also need two green candles and some matches. An optional prop to have nearby is a scepter or wand. Both Venus and Aphrodite are often depicted holding a scepter and a mirror, alluding to their aspects as Goddesses of both beauty and personal power.

If you are a woman who wears makeup on a regular basis or who enjoys playing or experimenting with makeup, have that on hand too. Just know that it is not required since true beauty does not come from a jar. Remember that Venus didn't have a Walgreens to run to when she felt a pimple coming on.

In the area you are working in, mentally cast a circle in which nothing but beauty may exist. Visualize this until it's real. This is your sacred space, a private place out of time and space where you alone decide what stays and what goes. Enter into this circle unclothed if possible, or in loose clothing such as a dressing gown or bath robe. Be clean, fresh from your shower, and with no makeup on your face at all.

Place the mirror on a surface where you can see your face without straining while you sit or stand before it. You want to be able to concentrate on the ritual aspects of this spell, not on maintaining your balance so you can see your reflection.

Take the green powder and rub some on the shaft of each candle, beginning the process at the candle's center and working outward. Don't slather it on, just wipe gently as you move your fingers from the center to both the top and base of each candle's shaft. Visualize the energy of the beauty of Venus adorning each candle and enhancing its magickal power.

When you are done powdering the candles, place them on either side of the mirror and light them. Be sure to keep them far enough away that you won't catch your hair on fire.

Gaze at your reflection as it is illuminated in the golden light of the candles. Almost all women look good in candlelight. Candlelight gives us a healthy glow, and it evens out skin tones and helps hide small flaws. In that way, candlelight is almost the ultimate beauty secret. This soft lighting will add a mysterious element to your ritual and help you accept that you, like Venus, are a true beauty.

As you gaze at your reflection, know without any doubt that all women—all people, in fact—have a beauty that dwells both inside and outside, and that cultural beauty standards are merely fads or control devices that do not affect the true beauty the Goddess granted her children. Know that it is your birthright to feel beauty is part of your overall package of self-esteem. Think back on the long lineage of women who helped create your looks: your mother, grandmothers, great-grandmothers, and on and on, back to the birth of humanity. They are all within you now; they helped make you. Were these women not beautiful? Did they have no value other than their appearance? Honor them with your confidence and pride. Know that it is your right to feel beautiful all the time, and you will feel your personal power surge.

If you happen to have a makeup collection on hand, you may start using it now, adding any enhancements you feel best supports the look you want to present to the world. With each stroke see Venus blessing your face with her essence of beauty and attraction.

Whether you are using makeup right now or not, you should be mentally conjuring up the image you want the world to see when they look at your face. Visualize it clearly in every detail. Make it so real that your reflection seems to transform itself as you gaze upon it, changing at your will.

Using a finger rather than a makeup applicator, touch first each candle shaft and then the green powder in the makeup compact while saying:

> *Venus, Goddess of all I see,*
> *Bless me now with beauty be;*
> *The visage I will is the face I wear,*
> *To scorn my looks no one will dare.*

Use your finger to swipe the green powder on each side of your neck and on the back of your neck. Feel the green color ignite the beauty of Venus within you. Gaze into the mirror and know that all the world sees you as beautiful.

> *Venus, as I magickally use your green,*
> *Or light the candles that remain unseen;*
> *I know your power to me does flow,*
> *I am beautiful wherever I go.*

Oh, Venus, bless me with beauty to behold;
Your fire draws attention as it did in days of old;
When I don the green or ignite the beauty's flame,
Venus grants me beauty, I ask this in her name.

Spend as much time as you like securing your image in the mirror before ending your ritual. If you have a scepter or wand on hand, you may want to touch it to your forehead and to your forehead's image in the mirror to seal the spell with this emblem of your personal power.

When you are done, extinguish the candles. Keep them and the powder compact covered somewhere away from prying eyes. Whenever you want to renew the spell, burn the candles or place some of the green powder on your body to draw on Venus' blessing of beauty.

The Creative Power of Isis

Isis is the mother Goddess of the Egyptian pantheon, consort to the God of life and death, Osiris. Her original name, Auset, means "supreme queen" or "spirit." Many scholars believe she is the prototype for all the Western mother Goddesses we still know today.

Isis is stern, but a nurturer; she holds the power of life and death, but she is compassionate; she loves her children, but is strict with them. She taught her people agriculture, spinning, and weaving. She blessed the water and vegetation that sprang forth from the deserts in the first year of Creation. She was skilled in magick and divination, and developed a reputation and following that flowed far beyond the borders of her native country.

Images of Isis that date back more than four thousand years can still be found on papyruses and bas relief carvings in modern Egypt. She is usually depicted as having winged arms. On her head are two bull's horns, images of the power of earth. The horns cradle a sun disc, an image of the power of the heavens. In one extant statue her horns are girdled, the girdle being used by Witches since ancient times as an emblem of personal power. In this same depiction she is draped with the serpent of magick known as the uraeus—a symbol of mother Goddesses and creative power—as she suckles her son, the child God Horus.

Isis's face is depicted as being adorned with a heavy hand. The popular image of Queen Cleopatra should conjure up for you an accurate mental image of how Isis's face was made up. In fact, Cleopatra was almost certainly trying to look like Isis to legitimize her rulership in the way most monarchs have done by claiming the throne as a divine right. Egyptian rulers were viewed not only as sons and daughters of the deities, but as their reincarnations. As such, they had to look the divine part more than many rulers.

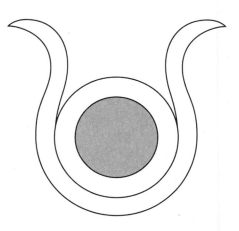

The crescent-shaped (bovine) Horn of Isis

156

In Egyptian art, black makeup is shown covering the eye area and extending out across the temples. Lip rouge is heavy, sharply outlining the lips. Cheekbones are highlighted to appear squarish and prominent. The jaw line is also highlighted to appear square and angular. The overall effect is one that is strong and determined, and a bit catlike.

Gold was the ornamentation of choice in ancient Egypt, but you may wish to add gemstones with magickal meaning or employ an ankh or scarab necklace or broach to help invoke the atmosphere this ritual seeks. The ankh is a symbol of life that dates to ancient Egypt, and the scarab is the beetle image that is used as a talisman of personal power and protection.

Plan ahead to decide how you can best make yourself into Isis incarnate so you can make a smooth transformation during your ritual.

The ankh

The Isis Ritual for Creative Power

This ritual requires using facial makeup—not in an attempt to have you conform with any modern-day beauty standard, but so your visage becomes as close to that of Isis as possible. It will be hard to get the full effect of this ritual without using makeup, but you're welcome to try.

For this ritual you will need to set up an altar in honor of Isis and all the mother Goddesses her visage inspired. This can be as simple as having a representation of some horns and a candle that you burn, both as a sacrifice to her and to represent the presence of her life force at your ritual. The candle's color should be your own choice. A stable pillar candle works best here to both symbolize Isis as the base of the mother Goddess archetype, and to enhance the safety factor while your focus is on making your transformation. Your altar may also display representations of mother Goddesses from the world over, or hold ritual tools, statuary, and incense, or it may display nothing else at all. Do what is most comfortable for you.

It is best to enact this ritual early during the third to fifth days of the waxing moon phase. Though we usually associate mother energy with the full moon, Isis is so strongly identified with horns—similar to most virgin Goddesses—that the natural horned symbol of the waxing moon helps us make a strong connection to her.

It is interesting to note that until at least the late Middle Ages the term "virgin" did not refer to a woman uninitiated in sexual intercourse. The Latin term from which the word derives, *virgo intactus*, did not refer to the hymen or skin covering the opening of the vagina in women who have not had sexual intercourse, but to being whole. A woman "intact" belonged only to herself. She was sovereign unto herself and free to make her own life's choices and to take any and all lovers she chose without fear of censor from society. The temple priestesses and prostitutes of ancient Rome, known as the Vestal Virgins, were examples of intact women in this sense. Considering this history it is not surprising that mother Goddesses would sport the horns of the virgin and be worshipped when the moon's horns grow like a belly in pregnancy during the waxing moon phase.

You will also need to have on hand a mirror the size and shape of your own choosing and all the clothing, jewelry, makeup, and other accoutrements you've chosen to make your transformation into Isis during this ritual.

When you are ready to begin, call your quarters and open your circle. For those of you new to magickal ritual, these terms refer to inviting the powers of the elements associated with the four cardinal directions to both assist and protect your circle or working area, and to evoke on it a protective and containing circular energy. The precise methods for doing this are presented in detail in most any book on Witchcraft or Pagan religious practice and should be consulted if you wish to continue working magickal rituals on a regular basis.

If you are a beginner, follow these steps to call your quarters and cast your circle. Do them in reverse order when the ritual is complete and you are ready to close the circle. While your circle is open, you must respect its boundaries and remember you are within sacred space. All your thoughts and actions are magnified three times during ritual.

1) Start your quarter call at any directional point you like: east, south, north, or west. All magickal traditions have those who believe their tradition's directional starting point is the only one possible. In truth, they all have been used at one time or another, depending on the type of ritual or magickal goal being enacted. No single starting point is better or worse than any other. What works best is what you feel is right for your particular spell or need.

2) Ask in your own words that the power of the elements be at your circle to bless, assist, and join in celebration. Don't make demands, but phrase your request as an invitation. Move clockwise around your working area, stopping at each cardinal point to make your invitation. The most common elemental associations for each direction come from modern eclectic Wicca, a widely popular Witchcraft tradition.

North	Earth
East	Air
South	Fire
West	Water

3) When you have arrived back at your starting directional point, take one more full clockwise walk around the circle while visualizing a wall or sphere of protective and containing energy rising around the area. You may wish to make more than one pass around the circle until you feel the circle's energy is strong.

Your circle is now open and the calling of the quarters is complete.

Stand where you have access to all your Isis accoutrements and where you can see yourself in the mirror. Offer a blessing to Isis, one that invites her to your circle.

Blessed be the Goddess of Creation,
Beloved to every Pagan nation;
Horned one, Isis, mother of all,
I beg you, please, to answer my call.
In my circle I ask you to be its heart,
Your creative energy to me impart;
I am your child, O mother, bless me,
As I will it now, so mote it be.

If you have not done so already, light your candle in honor of Isis.

Begin your transformation process with clothing and other accoutrements first, leaving your face until last. Watch yourself in the mirror as you start to become Isis and try to sense her blessing your ritual. Feel her melding with you in a oneness of spirit. This union is known in Pagan magickal circles as an invocation, a process in which the divine enters your being and changes it on all levels of existence.

Begin on your face when you are done with your clothing. As you do your Isis makeup, try to sense that you are seeing the world through her eyes. Imagine you are the powerful and revered Queen of Heaven and Earth. Feel her energy merge with your own, infusing you with divinity.

When you are done, ask Isis to give you the gift of her creative power. This will be useful for you both as a practitioner of magick and as a person who has to come up with creative solutions to everyday problems.

Isis, mother, Goddess kind,
Blessed be the creative mind;

continued . . .

159

This is the day and now is the hour,
Imbue me with your creative power.
Bless you, mother, for I am yours,
You close some windows, but open doors;
Let me always know the power is mine,
Creative solutions I can always find.
Blessed Isis, Goddess of love,
As below, so above;
By the power of three times three,
As I will, so mote it be.

When you are ready, thank and bless the elements as they depart, working around your circle in the reverse order in which you called them. Also thank and bless Isis for her assistance.

Walk counterclockwise around your circle to ground the energy you put in place during its creation. Visualize it being grounded.

Know that you have made a special connection with your first ancestor: Isis, the mother of us all. Know that you may call upon her power when you need creative energy for any reason, or when you want to project her beauty and power.

eight

The Glamoury

O fairest of creation! last and best
Of all God's works! creature in whom excell'd
Whatever can to sight or thought be formed.
—John Milton

Like it or not, the glamoury spell is all about looks. Its immediate goal, for better or for worse, is projecting a change in appearance. It may be one that you find desirable for attaining a specific goal above and beyond merely having people see you as you want them to see you. For example, you may need to project beauty to attract a mate, or project capability to attract a job, but the immediate glamoury goal is always looking the way you want to look in the eyes of others.

The glamoury is controversial. Is it a manipulative art? If and when it is manipulative, what possible need would be great enough to cause someone to resort to negative magick? If and when it is not manipulative, what justifies its use? Does the practitioner's outward appearance actually change or just the perception of it? Does the inner self change in response to the perception of the outer self? If so, is it a lasting change, as achieved with other forms of magick and ritual? Is the glamoury spell a dangerous, devilish practice, best avoided by those treading the spiritual path of "harm none"? Or is the glamoury just another useful tool in the arsenal of appearance magick?

These are questions only you can answer for yourself after thought and consideration. Only you will work the spell and only you will receive its benefits or backlashes.

A History of Mystery

Glamoury is illusion. It is magick culled from the realm of Europe's faery folk, who have long had the reputation of being able to appear in haunting and attractive guises to lure humans to their world. The glamoury falls in that category of transformational spells that evoke endless fascination in both practitioners and nonpractitioners of magick. Like other shapeshifting arts, such as that of taking on an animal form, the idea that a mere mortal—in particular, a woman—could alter her physical appearance at will both fascinated and horrified the old Witch hunters. Extant transcripts of Witch trials in both Europe and North America show the endless questioning women endured on this topic. The only other arts that drew as much interest from the inquisitors were those of summoning demons or the spirits of the dead and engaging in out-of-body travel or "flying."

The power of the glamoury spell was so scary to the men who both believed in the inherent evil of Witchcraft—as taught to them by their misinformed church leaders—and who held local political power that, in many places, meant laws were enacted that stated a man could divorce his new wife if he discovered after the wedding that she had used "artifice" to attract him and cause him to marry her. These laws remained on the books until at least the late nineteenth century, when they were interpreted as yet another reason, aside from modesty, that a woman should not wear makeup on her face. In other words, a woman who removed her makeup on her wedding night to the disillusionment of her new husband could be accused of using that makeup to lure him into the marriage, and the law said he was within his rights to seek divorce on these grounds.

The etymology of the word "glamoury" is telling as well. It comes from the French-speaking Normans, who brought it with them to England when they invaded and conquered in 1066 C.E. The word was originally used as a magickal term referring to a spell or enchantment. The term became applied to spells that created an illusion and, eventually, was applied solely to shapeshifting spells of a nonanimal nature. As the idea of using magickal artifice gripped the popular mind via Irish and Scottish legends of shapeshifting faery folk; and the word "glamorous" came into modern English, meaning to possess alluring looks or to fashion for oneself an irresistibly beautiful facade.

Note that a woman who is called glamorous is usually not also called a natural beauty, and that our conceptualization of her is still of one who flagrantly uses hair, makeup, and fashion tricks to achieve her end results. Sometimes this term conjures up an image of a woman who is overly made-up and tries too hard to look good. In this age where the appearance standard is one of seeking a natural look through artifice—a bizarre concept in itself when you think about it—the term glamourous is not always a positive adjective to apply to a woman.

The popular but sensationalized 1996 movie *The Craft* featured a glamoury spell that was simply referred to as a "glamour." By using it, the antagonist was able to take on the appearance of the protagonist in order to steal a wild moment with the protagonist's boyfriend. Hollywood's attention to over-the-top special effects made the transformation of the glamoury spell look like something it is not, yet it retained enough authenticity to confuse the mysterious spell further in the minds of both magickal and nonmagickal people.

Sexual enticement has always been implied in the glamoury, which has its roots deep in ancient Celtic myth and magick. In many cases, sexual attraction becomes the ultimate end goal of the spell. When the European tribes we know today as the Celts arrived in Ireland (between 1500 and 500 B.C.E.), mythology tells us they found the island inhabited by beautiful beings who called themselves the Tuatha De Danaan, or the Children of the Goddess Dana. The Tuatha were semidivine; fair, tall, solid-built, and undeniably sexually attractive. They seemed at one with the land, able to adapt to their surroundings and change their physical forms at will. They did not hesitate to appear even more attractive if they needed to in order to protect themselves from the invaders.

The Tuatha ultimately lost the battle for control of Ireland and went underground to become the mythic faery race of modern Ireland, the beings we refer to today in legends of the "hollow hills." For almost two thousand years Irish legends tell of faery beings who leave their underground burrows and appear to hapless humans in alluring guises to lead them into danger or capture them into the world of faery. This is the mysterious glamoury at work, and it is an art still practiced by modern magicians.

To make your glamoury work its best, you must remain realistic about what this spell can and cannot do. It will not make you take on the full, solid, physical body of another person so you can go out and fool people. At least it can't on the earth plane of existence, though it will work to some extent on the astral plane after you've gained experience in the art. Keep in mind that magick eventually translates into the earth realm but is viewed through the magickal reality of our other levels of awareness. A glamoury cannot make everyone who sees you fall madly in love with you, though it will draw to you more eyes than you ever expected. Almost no one will think you're not, at the very least, a very attractive woman. Finally, a glamoury cannot make you gain or lose weight or cure your acne, but it can be wonderful magickal support as you seek these goals.

Selecting a Glamoury Catalyst

The key to making the glamoury work is to choose a glamoury trigger, or catalyst, that you can wear inconspicuously on your person. Clothing and magickal perfumes have on occasion been chosen for this but both have drawbacks. Selecting a clothing catalyst would require you to wear the same outfit each time you wanted to work the glamoury spell, and perfume does not provide any visual focal point to help draw the eye to you. However, magickal perfumes can support the glamoury spell and boost its effectiveness. See chapter 6 for perfume recipe suggestions.

The best catalyst I've found for the glamoury spell is a piece of jewelry you like and can wear with almost anything. I find a necklace resting on bare skin works best since it draws the eye right to the heart area, near the center of your physical body.

When I worked with glamoury spells in the past, I used a small opal and diamond pendant on a thin gold chain as my catalyst. Gold gives the power of the sun, which is active energy. The diamonds have been associated with romance since the fifteenth century, when they became betrothal presents among royalty. Opals have a visual depth, one that you seem to be able to see into. They are also a stone that has been considered unlucky, similar to the number thirteen, because of their association with Witchcraft.

Bracelets draw the eye away from the body because arms move when we speak, walk, or even when we just sit. It doesn't provide a good focus. Earrings split visual focus and, though they draw attention up to the face, they don't put it on your center of being.

Though I don't sport one myself, a nose ring might work just as well as a necklace. If you wear one, you might consider using it as a glamoury trigger. It will draw the focus of the person or persons you are trying to attract to the center of your face and hold it in that one spot, similar to the way a necklace would draw attention to your heart center.

Don't rush to select your glamoury catalyst. You will put a lot of time and energy into its programing. This is not an easy spell to work, nor is it one usually attempted by magickal beginners or those who do not want to expend magickal effort over the long term. Make sure your catalyst is one that will work for you over and over again and that it draws attention where you want it without screaming "magick" at everyone who passes by.

The two spells that appear in this chapter are designed to increase the illusion of beauty, but be aware that glamoury spells have not always been used to make the physical appearance more lovely. On occasion they have been used to project a repellent appearance.

A glamoury can also be used to project the image of self-confidence, or strength, or weakness, depending upon your need at the time. You may create as many glamoury spells as you can focus upon at one time. Just remember that they all require their own catalysts, much effort, and an ongoing feed of energy. Your words of power must be chosen with care to avoid getting what you wish for but really don't want. Think it through with care before acting.

Jewelry Glamoury Spell

To create a glamoury spell with a piece of jewelry as a catalyst you will need a candle in either gold, red, orange, or green. Gold is projective and energizing. Red is for passion and is a projective color. Orange contains the power of attraction, and green is the color of Venus and beauty. You may use two small pillar or taper candles in two different colors. You will also need to have on hand the catalyst you've chosen, and a mirror of any size in front of which you can sit or stand comfortably for at least thirty minutes.

An optional item to have is an oil to use to anoint the catalyst. You may want to try jasmine or rosemary, or experiment with Anna Riva's Bewitching Oil, which is packaged and sold through International Imports of Los Angeles. Riva's products can be bought or ordered in most occult shops or through mail-order channels. See Appendix A for resources.

This spell will need to be repeated to maintain its energy. I recommend three times a week for the duration that you want the spell to be effective. After several months you can taper off to once a week, allowing the empowered catalyst to carry the load after that point.

This spell is best begun on the new moon and best performed at night, when deep shadows naturally distort physical reality. This helps your subconscious grasp the concept of shapeshifting and boosts the effectiveness of the spell. Because this is a spell of Celtic origin, it employs the energy of the Celtic sacred number of three. The words of power are spoken three times and the catalyst is anointed three times with oil. Look for other ways to employ the number three or, if you're really ambitious, use the number nine, the sacred multiple of three times three.

Before you start your glamoury spell, hold your chosen catalyst against the ground or under running water to allow all previous "programming" to be washed away. This occurs in any piece of jewelry, whether it was owned by a practitioner of magick or not. You don't want or need any conflicting energies in your spell. Spend as much time holding, wearing, and imprinting the energy of your spell's desired outcome into the catalyst as you possibly can.

When you are ready to begin the spell in earnest, get yourself comfortably in front of your mirror, with your lighted candles placed behind it or off to the sides so they do not shine directly on your reflection. I have used a wide dresser mirror for this spell that reflects me from the hips up. I find that moving the candles to the outside edge nearest me works best when I'm using my reflection for spellcrafting. Experiment to find the right combination of light and shadow to provide the right atmosphere for your spell.

Clasp your catalyst between both hands and project into it the image of what you want it to do for you. Gaze at your reflection in the mirror as you do this, making eye contact with yourself. See yourself becoming the image of beauty and attractiveness you seek to project to others.

If you have not spent any time beforehand holding your catalyst and feeding it the energy of your desire, you may need to spend upward of a half hour on this part of the spell alone. Don't be alarmed if during this time your reflection seems to be in motion, taking on a new character. This is a sign your spell is working.

Speak aloud the words of power whenever you feel ready. The quatrains that appear here should be read as a blueprint only. Just as you would look at house plans and make the adjustments that would make the final building a comfortable place for you to live, you should always adjust spells written by others to make them suitable to your personal use. The dictates of mass marketing means that spells you find in books such as these must be more generic in nature than you may need to be successful. Weigh each word you choose with care, consulting an oracle such as the tarot cards or runes if needed to make sure that the outcome you desire is what you will get.

> *From the hollow hills my power flows,*
> *By the Tuatha, my will it grows;*
> *By their beauty I cull my face,*
> *Ever reflecting beauty and grace.*
>
> *A face that conforms to my will, I dare,*
> *It is now the face I wear;*
> *Irresistible to all I must be,*
> *All eyes now find they're drawn to me.*
>
> *Beauty and charm with visual appeal,*
> *Positive attention I do steal;*
> *Infatuated by this glamoury of which I hold the key,*
> *This spell makes them see what I want them to see.*

Lightly anoint your chosen catalyst after speaking the words of power. Hold the catalyst up before your face. Laugh, sing, dangle the trinket in front of your charming face and feel the spell working. Gaze at yourself in the mirror and feel the pull of your attraction growing stronger. Cock your head with a flirtatious air. Laugh with insouciance. Let your eyes dance and sparkle. This is the moment where the glamoury first starts to take shape and begins the path to manifestation. Allow the spell to take the self-image of your fondest imagination from the world of the unformed. From here you will pull it right from the mirror into the world of form for all to see.

Sometimes it helps to visualize the look you want working its way from the unseen world by gaining in density as it passes through the elements. Visualize the looks you want moving from the unseen world into the world of the elements of air. With air it takes on the power of movement and the power to invade the thoughts of others. As it gains in density on its way to manifestation it passes into the element of fire, where it picks up the power of transformation and passion. Passing into the world of water, your image absorbs the energies of love and mystery. The last world it passes through on its way to the physical world is the realm of earth, where it gains in solidity and projects the air of stability and reliability.

At this point you should repeat again the words of power. Intone them with a clear and sure voice. Anoint the catalyst again after speaking the words of power.

Place the catalyst on your body as you will wear it when you are out where others can see you. Wearing the catalyst is the easiest way to trigger the glamoury spell later on. When you wear it, it will pull over you the veil of illusion, the glamoury. Look in the mirror and see it happen right now and know that it will also happen when you're out among others.

As you gaze at your desired reflection, repeat the words of power one last time. Anoint the catalyst one last time after speaking them.

Whenever you want to project this glamoury image of yourself to the world, you should don the talisman and repeat the words of power, whether to yourself or aloud. Do this anywhere, anytime you need to, but try not to look conspicuous. Fortunately it is not uncommon for a woman to grasp a necklace in her hands when she is out. You should feel a burst of inner power after you speak your words of power. Let it give you confidence that the spell is working and drawing all eyes to your devastating beauty.

You should also do whatever you can in the physical world to make yourself more attractive to others. This does not mean you should be a slave to popular fashion or try to be anyone other than the person you are. It just means you might remember to smile more often, to listen better, or to be more confident. All of these are commonsense actions that make us attractive to other people and back up our magickal efforts.

An Anglo-Saxon Circular Glamoury

I first learned about the powerful circular spells of Anglo-Saxon origin several years ago from Pagan author Patricia Monaghan. She had found them very successful, and my own experiments have shown me that they seem to evoke a potent form of "be careful what you wish for" energy.

Circular spells are constructed in a way that the goal of the spell appears to have no beginning and no end. One statement is made that results in an action, which results in an action, which results in another, and on and on until the actions return you to the original statement from the first line. The concept is a wonderful one for Pagan practitioners of magick who understand and accept the circular nature of cause and effect within nonlinear time.

A circular spell can be used for any need, but when used in a glamoury spell I find it still works best in tandem with a jewelry catalyst. In the case of circular spells you may want to use a trigger with a circular image to help you connect with the visual concept of the spell.

I have discovered through experimentation that a circular spell with thirteen actions produces the most potent results; the thirteenth action looping back into the first. Naturally this is no more a requirement for a successful circular spell than having thirteen people is required for a successful coven, but you should keep the idea in mind. The completion of your thoughts is what will work best. If you can mold it into thirteen steps, great; if not, that's fine too. Note that with thirteen steps you will have either fourteen or twenty-eight lines, depending on if you use two lines per step or one. This has no affect on the magick, it's merely to make the rhyme scheme flow: fourteen single lines or seven couplets, or twenty-eight single lines or seven quatrains.

Again, keep in mind the blueprint nature of a spell written for the mass market by someone else. The circular spell should make sense to your life and situation to be most effective. For example, the one I used with great success employs lines about dancing. I'm a ballroom dancer and I'm most likely to find myself in dance settings when I want to use the glamoury to attract an unending string of good partners, since the women usually outnumber the men. The image of being seen as an attractive woman and a skilled dancer makes my glamoury more effective than if I intoned only generic lines that basically say no more than, "I look real good and you will not be able to help but notice." That alone wouldn't help me achieve my true end goal of having men dance with me.

Notice that I had a specific goal in mind—having many dance partners—when I created my spell. For best results, you should have a clear goal, too. You may be seeking a romantic partner, new friends, or you may just need to be projecting confidence to land a job or impress a new man in your life. Whatever your desire, make it as specific as you can. You must have your goal firmly in mind when you create any spell if you want it to work its best.

Several years ago when I was living in Texas I knew a woman who was having trouble creating love spells that worked. She asked me to review her spell to see if I could find out why it wasn't working. The spell asked for a specific married man to notice her and be interested in her. She told me he seemed intrigued by her, and she'd caught him gazing at her repeatedly throughout the day in the place where they worked together. She couldn't understand why he had made no effort to initiate a relationship with her. I told her it was probably a twofold problem. First of all, his bond with his wife and family could have been stronger than her magick and, in the second place, the spell asked for his attention and no more. She had gotten exactly what she asked for. The spell had worked.

As with the other glamoury spell in this chapter, repeat it weekly and when you need to renew its energy.

1   *I'm here for all the world to see,*
2   *All want to know the beauty that is me.*
3   *Beauty calls them to look my way,*

4	*When looking my way they want to stay,*
5	*Stay at my side and gaze at my face,*
6	*A face of beauty that smiles with grace,*
7	*Grace that sends a message clear,*
8	*I'm someone they have to be near,*
9	*The nearer they come the more they feel,*
10	*My power their hearts and mind do steal,*
11	*I steal the looks and the attention of all,*
12	*Attention to my beauty, my siren call,*
13	*A siren song born of this spell,*
14	*That all who see me love me well, as . . .*

When you reach the final line of the words of power you should begin the first line again. One flows into the other, making a never-ending chain of events that trigger the glamoury spell.

A Glamoury Love Spell

I once read a bit of wisdom that taught that women fall in love through what they hear and men fall in love through what they see. Whether that's a difference native to our different brain structures or something taught to us by society is not clear. Perhaps it's not even true, but the fact remains that the way we appear to others has a lot to do with the first impression they form of us, and men seem to be more concerned than women about the physical packaging of a potential romantic partner.

This fact does not mean you should rush out and immediately try to mold yourself into the image of this week's hottest fashion model. We all have different tastes in body style and coloring and there is always someone, somewhere, who will think yours is perfect.

The glamoury works well in combination with love magick because it first seeks to make an irresistible attraction which, in a romantic situation, can be turned into a new relationship.

One of the trickiest part of constructing any spell is walking the fine line between being specific about what you want while not dictating to or blocking the powers of the universe from bringing it to you in the best way possible. Like all other movement of energy, magickal energy will follow the path of least resistance. We aren't always able to see what that might be. On the other hand, we need to make our intentions clear in both our words and our mental imagery.

The next example of words of power for a glamoury spell is more specific. It is designed to draw the attention of the right person at a dance or a nightclub. Most of us who seek a mate do so with the hope that he or she will enjoy the same activities we do, and to that end we seek that special person all the harder when at an activity we really love. Whether you love to dance, go clubbing, sing, show dogs, surf, ski, read, write, play chess, volunteer, collect stamps, play in a symphony, or anything else you could imagine doing with your leisure time, try constructing your glamoury spell for that specific event just to see who you might attract.

At the risk of sounding like an obsessive-compulsive, keep in mind that aiming this spell at a specific person is manipulative magick that violates free will and will eventually backfire on you.

1   *From across the room your eyes mine greet,*
2   *You cross to me so we can meet;*
3   *You meet me and you think me fair,*
4   *Unknowingly drawn into my lair.*

5   *Within my lair you want to stay,*
6   *I enchant you as the fey;*
7   *And by the fey this spell I make,*
8   *That your heart my own does take.*

9   *Faster your heart beats, you feel so much,*
10   *You beg me dance, you crave my touch;*
11   *We move as one to a haunting tune,*
12   *My spell now blessed by mother moon.*

13   *As with moon madness your senses run,*
14   *You wonder if I could be "the one";*
15   *And your wonderings make you sigh,*
16   *I can see the question in your eye.*

17	*You question if again see me you may,*
18	*And I tell you only to pick the day;*
19	*As days go by my spell grows strong,*
20	*You do not think we can go wrong.*

21	*With no sense of wrong our love is sown,*
22	*Our passions bloom, our relationship grown;*
23	*Our relationship to you is dear,*
24	*You love me well and without fear.*

25	*Without fear the way is free,*
26	*For you and me in love to be;*
27	*And all because you felt the thrill,*
28	*As you saw me there and fell under my spell . . .*

Cultivating Eye-Catching Appeal

It only makes sense to close out a book on appearance magick with a miscellany of commonsense, albeit somewhat scientific, suggestions on how to be your eye-catching best. Think of this section as the final step in glamoury spellcraft: working in the physical world to assist your magick to manifest.

Trite it may be, it remains true that those who project an air of self-confidence and friendliness attract others. This includes both friends and lovers. Appearing self-confident requires no more than holding your head up and adopting good posture. When we stand tall we are perceived by others as proud and in control.

The aura of friendliness can be projected with what I call the Threefold Friend-Finding Formula:

Step 1: Smile

A smile is your personal people magnet. It can draw eyes to you from clear across a football field. A genuine smile relaxes your face and projects an open, approachable image to everyone. A dazzling enough smile can open more doors for you than slipping 100 dollars to a starving doorman. A slightly open-mouthed smile is registered by most people as an indication of sexual interest in another person and can help signal a new man that you're very interested in knowing him better.

Step 2: Listen

Most of us talk too much . . . *way* too much. When you're trying to meet new friends or lovers, make a point of talking less and listening more. People will love you for it and seek you out in crowds because you put them at ease and make them feel good about themselves.

Lean your upper body forward slightly while listening, and make good eye contact. This body language lets the other person know you're really interested in what he or she has to say. Refrain from crossing your arms over your chest. This gesture gives the impression of impatience and defensiveness.

Ask open-ended questions rather than those that require only a yes or no answer. This gives someone you're interested in a chance to converse with you. Conversation is the only way either of you will know for sure if you want to pursue a relationship beyond the moment. If you have trouble making small talk, these open-ended questions take the burden off you by allowing the other person to talk about him or herself, something most people love to do. Questions such as "That's an unusual job. What's your average day like?" or "You make me laugh. What were you like in school?" can get someone you're interested in knowing better off on a monologue.

Another trick to making conversation is to wear or have a conversation piece handy, such as an unusual piece of jewelry or an offbeat item perched on your desk. These things arouse curiosity in others and provoke questions. They also provide a topic of conversation for strangers that's more compelling than the day's weather.

Step 3: Touch

Touch stimulates the hormones that bond us to one another and makes us feel someone wants to bump the budding relationship up to a more intimate level. Touching doesn't meaning pawing someone else or being so touchy-feely that you invade their personal space. There are some people who don't like to be touched by anyone but those in their most intimate inner circle.

A touch needs to be no more than a pat on the shoulder when you part, a squeeze of the hand while you dance, or a quick pat of the hand on someone's forearm when making a conversational point. These can all convey your real interest in the other person that is not threatening and does invade their sense of personal space.

Don't forget to make eye contact. Eye contact is a form of touch Americans have not cultivated. People feel you're more honest when you meet their eyes and, when a gaze is held just a little longer than is customary, it usually signals romantic interest on your part.

When seeking to make intimate connections with others it should go without saying that you always appear in public clean and well-groomed. This isn't the same as wearing a strong cologne to cover a little body odor or wearing lots of makeup or sporting an elaborate hairstyle. Those things do not make lasting impacts, at least not the kind of impact you seek. They can even be a turnoff. A clean body, brushed teeth, and combed hair will make a better impression.

Your clothing should be tasteful and appropriate to the arena in which you find yourself. In other words, evening gowns on an afternoon shopping trip or bikinis at a business meeting are not recommended. Indulge your individuality with accessories and color choices instead.

Bold accessories are perceived as belonging to bold people. Small, delicate, classic accessories scream sophistication. Too many accessories say you're tacky; too few that your self-image needs a boost or that you like your freedom. Gold and silver accessories catch the eye best in soft lighting.

The colors you choose to wear will also convey an impression of you to others. While you should always choose colors that work best with your skin tone and complexion, certain shades will broadcast to others a lasting image of who you are.

Red. Red makes a bold impact. It stimulates the senses and projects ultimate self-confidence and creates its own energy. Red catches the eye. The more red in your outfit, the bolder and more forceful you are perceived as being. Shades of red you can experiment with to discover which looks best with your coloring are: ruby, garnet, maroon, crimson, scarlet, blood, burgundy, raspberry, garnet.

Blue. Blue is the opposite of red. Blue is calming and those who wear it are viewed as stable and reliable. Too much of it can be depressing. Blue recedes and, without a bold accent piece, wearing it can cause you to recede into the background. On the plus side, wearers of blue are viewed as loyal and steadfast. Almost anyone can look good in some shade of blue: turquoise, periwinkle, azure, cerulean, navy, aqua, royal, baby, sapphire, cobalt.

Black. Black is the evening wear classic that never goes out of style. Black fabric hides flaws in workmanship and conceals cheaper fabrics. It conveys an aura of mystery and sophistication in women past their twenties. If black is too severe for your coloring, try experimenting with softer blacks: gray, silver, charcoal.

Green. Green is a color of the earth. It is reliable, trustworthy, and calming. It is traditional for actors to await the curtain rising on their shows from a room hued in green to help quell stage fright. Wearers of green are seen as traditional and balanced people. Greens are usually shaded with blues (cool tones) or yellows (warm tones) and it can be tricky to find the one that looks best on you. Shades to experiment with are: kelly, hunter, forest, grass, lime, chartreuse, teal, pine, jade, olive, pea, malachite, apple, sea, emerald, peridot.

Pink. Pink is really soft red associated with youth and beauty. Softer pinks are perceived as girlish and, often, too cute. Those who sport bolder, brighter pinks are viewed as risk takers and as being bold themselves. Shade of pink include: baby, watermelon, mauve, rose, hot.

Yellow. Bright yellows convey a sunny disposition and the more muted shades are seen as a shield for hidden vivacity. Those who wear yellow are seen as intelligent. Shades of yellow include: gold, lemon, mustard, topaz, canary, honey.

Brown. Brown is another earthly shade, usually classed as a neutral rather than as a color in clothing terms. Unrelieved browns can look mousy and dull, and those characteristics can be projected onto the wearer. Those who wear brown without imaginative clothing cuts or accessories are sometimes viewed as fearful or afraid of taking risks. There are many shades of brown that can compliment your own coloring without making you appear washed out, particularly the shades with golden undertones. Experiment with browns by different names: beige, camel, honey, sienna, mahogany, bronze, coffee, chocolate, taupe, putty, tan, ginger, mocha, cafe au lait, toffee.

Orange. Brownish shades of orange are viewed as trustworthy and earthy while the bolder tones are seen as belonging to someone who is racy and outgoing. It can convey qualities of leadership and friendliness. Orange comes in a broad range of shades and hues: coral, cayenne, apricot, peach, burnt, rust, salmon, tangerine, pumpkin, terra cotta, carnelian, copper.

White. Surprise! White is not viewed as a virginal color or one associated with only brides. White fabrics of good quality are seen as sporty and comfortable, classic and youthful. Wearers of white are viewed as versatile and team players. If you've ever gone shopping for white wall paint, you will have already discovered the vast range available. A white can be tinted or shaded with absolutely any other color—warm or cool—to correspond to any skin or hair coloring: ivory, ecru, candlelight, oyster, pearl, bone, cream, blue, winter, milk, snow.

Purple. Wearers of purple are perceived as unique characters: trendy and uninhibited, spiritual and creative, quirky and open, but sometimes self-absorbed. Purple is still viewed by many as a regal color, a shade donned by European royalty. Shades of purple include: violet, amethyst, indigo, plum, lavender, orchid, lilac, magenta, wine, eggplant, grape.

What you wear and how you wear it will always depend on your lifestyle and tastes, and you should always feel free to express yourself through the clothing, makeup, and other appearance choices you make. Beauty is subjective, and the various methods by which it is pursued are personal and as dear to each of us as the choices we make about our spiritual practices or sexual lifestyles.

You are beautiful by virtue of existing, just as you are magick. Enhance them both as you will.

The Blessing of Being

By the power of fire, be magickal.
By the power of water, be beautiful.
By the power of earth, be who you are.
By the power of air, be all you wish to be.
By the power of the Goddess, so mote it be.

appendix a
Resources

Local occult supply shops should always be checked into first for finding magickal accoutrements. This not only helps support other members of your community, but these shops are good places to find regional items unavailable or hard to find elsewhere. Another point in their favor is that they are usually good forums for getting to know other people living in your area who share your interests.

Many of these businesses and publications—and others like them—now have a presence on the Internet. This is another source for ordering supplies, inquiring about subscription rates, or perusing the editorial slant of a publication. Use your browser's search engines to find anything magickal. I experimented with putting in the words "rosemary oil" and got hundreds of hits for information, medicine, magick, and vendors. Most of us are already aware that not all resources online are accurate or honest. Be cautious about which businesses you give your credit card information to. Make sure the site is secure and uses SSL encription to protect your transactions.

Every attempt has been made to make this appendix accurate at the time of publication, but remember that addresses can change suddenly, businesses can fail, and periodicals can cease publication. Sometimes free catalogs find they must charge for subscriptions or raise prices to stay competative. If you are reading this book a year or more from its publication date, it would be wise to query business contacts with return postage to check on prices and the availability of goods and services. All prices are quoted in U.S. dollars unless otherwise stated. Always remember to enclose an SASE (self-addressed stamped envelope) whenever making inquiries to businesses within your own country, or an IRC (international reply coupon) when querying elsewhere. This is not only a matter of courtesy, but is often the only way to ensure a reply.

Herbs, Oils, and Other Accoutrements

Aroma Vera
5901 Rodeo Road
Los Angeles, CA 90016

Write for the catalog price on essential oils, floral waters, dried products, aromatherapy oils, and incense censers.

Azure Green
P.O. Box 48
Middlefield, MA 01243-0048
413-623-2155
http://www.azuregreen.com

Azure Green has almost everything, including Anna Riva's oil blends. Request a free catalog or order via their website.

Balefire
6504 Vista Ave.
Wauwatosa, WI 53213

This mail order company carries a large stock of brews, oils, and incenses designed for specific needs such as scrying, spirit contact, and spellwork. Write for a catalog.

Brambleberry
Bay Street Village, Space 11-12
301 W. Holly Street
Bellingham, WA 98225
360-738-8382
http://www.brambleberry.com

For oils, glycerin, soap molds, and product containers.

Capriland's Herb Farm
Silver Street
Coventry, CT 06238

Write for a free price list of dried herbs and herbal books. Capriland also holds special classes on herb use and has herbal lunches at various times throughout the year. Reservations are a must.

Cranberry Lane
65-2710 Barnet Highway
Coquitlam, BC V3B-1B8 Canada
604-944-1488
http://www.cranberrylane.com

Natural beauty product ingredients such as oils, dyes, preservatives, glycerin, molds, and product containers.

Dreaming Spirit
P.O. Box 4263
Danbury, CT 06813-4263

Natural, homemade incenses and resins, oils, and tools for using them. Dreaming Spirit welcomes queries about custom blends of incenses or oils. The $2 for their catalog is refundable with your first order.

Earth Scents by Marah
Box 948
Madison, NJ 07940
Sellers of herbs, incenses, books, oil blends, and other tools. Catalog, $1.

Gypsy Heaven
115 S. Main St.
New Hope, PA 18938
(215) 862-5251
Request a catalog of magickal supplies. Currently their catalog is being offered for free, but it doesn't hurt to check this information.

Halcyon Herb Company
Box 7153 L
Halcyon, CA 93421
Sells not only magickal herbs, but also staffs, brooms, cloaks, drums, and other items of interest to Pagan folk. Current catalog, $5.

Indiana Botanic Gardens
2401 W. 37th Avenue
Hobart, IN 46342
http://www.botanichealth.com
Sells herbal health products, dried herbs, and essential oils.

International Imports
236 W. Manchester Ave.
Los Angeles, CA 90003
Write for information on obtaining a catalog. This company makes and sells Anna Riva's oils and powders, and several books on magick of a negative but informative nature.

Lavendar Folk Herbal
P.O. Box 1261, Dept. SW
Boulder, CO 80306
Medicinal and magickal tea blends, herbs, and herbal crafts. $2 catalog is refundable with first order.

Leydet Oils
P.O. Box 2354
Fair Oaks, CA 95628

Sellers of fine essential oils. Price list is $2 as of this writing.

Light and Shadows
Catalog Consumer Service
2215-R Market St., Box 801
San Francisco, CA 94114-1612

Write for their free metaphysical supply catalog, or fire up your search engines and check out their website.

Moon Scents and Magickal Blends, Inc.
P.O. Box 1588-C
Cambridge, MA 02238

Large collection of magickal paraphernalia and books. Request a free catalog.

Natural Impulse Handmade Soap and Sundries
P.O. Box 94441
Birmingham, AL 35220
http://www.naturalimpulse.com

Sells ready-made soaps made of natural oils by a company openly committed to protecting the enviroment.

POTO
11002 Massachusetts Ave.
Westwood, CA 90025-3510
(310) 575-3717

POTO is short for "Procurer of the Obscure." Their mail-order catalog features services, and rare books and herbs for those in the magickal life. Special orders and requests always welcome. Send $5 for current catalog and ordering information.

Pourette
P.O. Box 15220
Seattle, WA 98115

Soapmaking and candlemaking supplies, including unscented gel, solid soap bases, and castile soap.

Sacred Spirit Products
P.O. Box 8163
Salem, MA 01971-8163

Sellers of books, magickal tools, herbs, incense, and other occult items. Catalog, $3.

Bottles and Containers for Magickal Potions

Sunburst Bottle Company
5710 Auburn Blvd., Suite 7
Sacramento, CA 95841

Bottle and container provider whose current catalog is $2. Write for current price.

General Bottle Supply
1930 E. 51st Street
Los Angeles, CA 90058

Write for free catalog of herb, oil, and salt bottles.

General Pagan Publications

Accord
Council of the Magickal Arts, Inc.
P.O. Box 890526
Houston, TX 77289

Published by a well-known Texas-based networking organization. As of this writing, sample issues are $4.50.

Blessed Bee
P.O. Box 641
Port Arena, CA 95468
707-882-2052
info@blessedbee.com

Publications for Pagan families with younger children. Call or e-mail for rates.

Circle
P.O. Box 219
Mt. Horeb, WI 53572
http://www.circlesanctuary.org

A popular, professional journal for Pagan news and gatherings, contacts, and seasonal celebration information. Sample copy, $5. Write for other subscription information.

The Green Egg
P.O. Box 1542
Ukiah, CA 95482
http://www.caw.org.green-egg

This very popular magazine has been around for a long time. Professionally formatted and always controversial. Contains beautiful artwork. Write for current rates.

Hecate's Loom
Box 5206, Station B
Victoria, BC
V8R 6N4
Canada

Another professional quality journal. Focus on Pagan arts. Write for rates. United States residents should include an IRC to ensure a reply.

Pangaia
Blessed Bee, Inc.
P.O. Box 641
Point Arena, CA 95468-0099
http://www.pangaia.com

Earth-focused general Pagan publication. Professional format and artwork.

appendix b
Interactions and Side Effects

As with anything concerning magick, the practitioner is urged to investigate all aspects of the spell, including the magickal correspondences, history, and pharmacology of the herbs that will be used. This appendix attempts to address some of the more common side effects of the plants and herbs used in the recipes in this book. While it certainly doesn't pretend to cover every eventuality or address the personal sensitivities of the reader, it can provide some insight when selecting natural ingredients for your bath and beauty magick.

The side effects that appear here are taken from data on plant and herb extracts that have been ingested, but please note that the extracts can enter your bloodstream by being absorbed through skin. This is why the warning bears repeating that women who are pregnant or nursing should leave most herbal products alone. This is also true for anyone with a medical condition in which common sense would contraindicate the use of a particular natural substance. There are many, many ways to create magick without having to put yourself at risk. It's just not worth it to take a chance.

Alfalfa. The seeds should never be used or consumed. They are poisonous and can interfere with red blood cell production.

Allspice. The dried herb is safe but the oil is a potent poison. Never ingest this or any other essential oil.

Aloe. Though touted as a great balm for skin irritations and burns, it has been linked to uterine contractions. Pregnant women should avoid using aloe.

Angelica. This herb can cause photosynthetic reactions on the skin when exposed to the sun. The fresh roots are a strong poison, but when dried they are tolerated. In the wild, angelica looks like several other plants that are extremely poisonous, and it should only be harvested by expert botanists.

Anise. Contrary to popular belief, anise and licorice are not the same substance. Anise is generally considered safe for consumption but licorice has been linked to hormonal imbalances and other neurochemical disturbances.

Apples. The meat and peel of an apple are fine to eat or use on your hair and skin, but the seeds contain cyanide and are highly poisonous.

Basil. Has been shown to contain both carcinogenic and anticarcinogenic properties.

Bay. Oil is toxic.

Bayberry. Contains tannins, which have been linked to stomach cancers. Bayberry root has been shown to have some medicinal uses but, as with all essential oils, bayberry oil should never be ingested.

Black Cohosh. This herb contains estrogen, a female hormone. It is also cardioactive and should be avoided by anyone with a cardiopulmonary disease.

Black Walnut Hulls. Sometimes used in natural hair rinses for very dark hair, these hulls stain skin and fabrics and are not recommended for cosmetic use.

Blackberry. Blackberry tea has been shown to constrict blood vessels when used in large amounts. It also contains tannins, which may cause stomach cancers or give a brown tint to blonde hair.

Boneset. The fresh herb is toxic and should never be used. Dried boneset is still considered an herb of "undefined safety."

Buckthorn. Can cause severe cramping if ingested.

Burdock. Considered an herb of "undefined safety." Burdock should be home-grown or purchased from a reputable source. Tainted herbs have been sold that have caused atropine poisoning.

Celandine. Used often in spells to open locks or offer protection but is highly poisonous.

Chamomile. This popular herbal tea ingredient is a cousin of ragweed and may cause the same severe reactions in sensitive individuals who use it either internally or externally.

Chicory. Contains tannins, which have been linked to stomach cancers. May irritate stomach lining.

Cinnamon. The oil is a potent skin irritant and it should never be ingested.

Cinquefoil. A mild poison.

Clove. Clove oil is a skin irritant and a poison when ingested. Never ingest this or any other essential oil. Though it has been touted as an antioxidant, even the dried herb can be rough on the stomach.

Coltsfoot. The tea has been proven to narrow blood vessels and should be avoided by anyone with heart disease or high blood pressure. It has also been suspected of causing liver damage. The U.S. Food and Drug Administration classes coltsfoot as an herb of "undefined safety."

Comfrey. Comfrey has also been thought to cause liver damage and is linked to some cancers. The U.S. FDA classes comfrey as an herb of "undefined safety."

Cowslip. Has qualities similar to chlorine bleach. Keep away from fabrics.

Cream of Tartar. When cream of tartar ferments it produces sulfites, just like in wines. Those with serious allergies to sulfites or sulfa drugs should be cautious when using cream of tartar, or avoid it altogether.

Damiana. Damiana is cardioactive. Avoid it if you have heart disease or high blood pressure.

Dill. May cause photosynthetic reaction.

Elecampane. May cause uterine contractions and should be avoided by pregnant women.

Eucalyptus Oil. As much as an ingested teaspoon of the oil has been fatal. Can cause stomach cramps. Recommended for small medicinal amounts only by those who are familiar with its properties.

Fennel. Contains estrogen, a female hormone. The seeds are safe but the oil is an extreme skin irritant. Taken internally, the oil is toxic.

Fenugreek. Contains a stimulant similar to caffeine and causes extreme stomach discomfort if small medicinal amounts are exceeded. Can cause uterine contractions and should not be used by pregnant women.

Ginger. Should not be used by those with blood-clotting disorders as it seems to act as an anticoagulant.

Goldenseal. Some studies of this herb have shown that it may cause unpredictable fluctuations in blood pressure and uterine contractions.

Gotu Kola. Though used frequently to treat wounds and improve circulation, gotu kola has been linked to unpleasant rashes and perhaps even skin cancers.

Hawthorn. Has been used as both a sedative and a heart stimulant. It has been shown to cause dramatic drops in blood pressure, leading to loss of consciousness. Tastes bitter and is best treated as a poison if ingested.

Lemon. The oil causes photosynthetic reactions. Don't use it on your skin before sun exposure.

Lily of the Valley. Great in love spells but highly, dangerously poisonous.

Madder Root. A good rinse for redheads but can stain skin and fabrics. Use in moderation.

Meadowsweet. This popular magickal herb has been known to cause uterine contractions and should not be used by pregnant women.

Mistletoe. This is a popular magickal herb in spite of the fact parts of it are poisonous. Most of the herb is cardioactive. Use with caution and keep away from children and pets.

Mullein. The seeds are poisonous. The dried herb contains tannins, which have been linked to stomach cancers.

Myrrh. When ingested it is an unpleasantly strong laxative, even a dangerous one. Myrrh been known to cause rapid heartbeat or, worse, life-threatening cardiac arrhythmias.

Nutmeg. Many people are surprised to find that the common cooking spice nutmeg is a poison. As much as one whole clove is enough to kill the average human being. The highly concentrated essential oil of nutmeg should be used with caution.

Papaya. Generally safe but has been known to cause allergic reactions.

Parsley. A potent diuretic. Long-term use of parsley to treat bad breath can deplete essential body salts.

Passionflower. This plant has been known to cause uterine contractions and should not be used by pregnant women.

Peppermint. Most of us would never consider that peppermint oil could be harmful, but when mixed with menthol it can be toxic if used in excess by those not trained to know how much is too much.

Psyllium. The seeds are popular as a mild laxative and are used by many to help maintain bowel regularity. It has been known to cause allergic reactions and to block the esophagus if taken improperly. It has also been known to cause uterine contractions and should not be used by pregnant women.

Red Clover. Contains estrogen, a female hormone. Also a potent source of iron and vitamin C.

Rose. Rich in vitamin C and a popular skin care treatment. Has been known to cause kidney problems and diarrhea.

Rosemary. The oil can be toxic in large doses. It has been known to cause problems for those with high blood pressure or epilepsy. Avoid rosemary if you have either of these conditions.

Saffron. This costly herb has been linked to uterine contractions and should not be used by pregnant women. The oil is not available commercially now, but good decoctions can be made from the dried herb.

Sage. The oil can be toxic and has been known to cause convulsions. Should not be used on fair hair.

St. John's Wort. Though sold over the counter as a very mild antidepressant, this herb is toxic when used in higher doses. This herb can cause dangerous interactions with alcohol and other drugs, just like the MAO inhibitors once popular in the medical treatment of depression. If you take this herb internally, don't exceed the manufacture's recommended dosage. Consult a physician or qualified botanist for guidance if you are the least bit unsure.

Skullcap. The Food and Drug Administration classes skullcap as an herb of "undefined safety." Experiment with caution.

Tarragon. This herb has caused tumors in laboratory animals.

Thyme. Thyme oil is an extreme skin irritant and is toxic in large amounts.

Turmeric. Should not be used by people with blood-clotting disorders, as it is a strong anticoagulant.

Valerian. A strong sedative that is toxic in large doses. Though sometimes used as an herbal sleeping aid, researchers are still divided on whether it is an addictive substance or not.

Vervain. Depresses the heartbeat. It has also been shown to constrict bronchial tubes and should not be used by anyone with cardiovascular disease, asthma, or severe respiratory allergies.

Yarrow. A popular magickal herb that is generally safe, but may cause an allergic reaction in people who are allergic to ragweed.

Yerba Maté. Teas made from yerba maté—generally just referred to as maté—are as popular as coffee in parts of South America but, like tea, it contains tannins, which have been suspected of causing stomach cancers.

Yerba Santa. Contains tannins, which have been linked to stomach cancers.

appendix c
FAQs (Frequently Asked Questions)

Interest in magick and Witchcraft has grown far beyond what I could have imagined when I first begin my study toward initiation in 1980. Today's seekers, like those of the past, are sincere, creative people who seek harmony with the universe and a path to the God and Goddess that makes sense to them within that harmony, and I have loved meeting with and hearing from everyone who has taken the time to write or to stop and introduce themselves. I have learned from everyone too. In the Craft we never stop being students and we are all teachers, whether we realize it or not.

This rising interest in Witchcraft also means that I receive more mail than I could hope to keep up with.

When I first began writing about Witchcraft I committed myself to personally answering each letter I received, remembering the days when I also needed to reach out to someone who might have some suggestions for me. The effort to keep up this commitment grew more difficult with the increased volume and, eventually, I was reduced to a form letter with a brief personal line at the bottom, which I found very uninspiring. Fortunately, there are alternatives.

Today there are experienced magicians, Witches, Wiccans, and Pagans in almost every city and town across North America, and plenty in Western Europe too. There are excellent books, groups, periodicals, and other resources that were only a dream even a decade ago. Many people who operate occult shops or metaphysical bookstores have been in the Craft for many years and can help answer your questions or can recommend books and resources for study. In other words, you have hundreds of resources to turn to for assistance, many that are faster and easier to reach than you might think.

Don't overlook the Internet as a source of networking and information. There are websites, chat rooms, news groups, vendors, periodicals, and a host of other links that explore magick and Paganism from every angle and viewpoint. If you do not own a computer, your local library or public university probably has one you can use for free to browse the Internet. Try plugging keywords into the browser's search engine such as magic(k), Pagan, Wicca, and Witchcraft for a slew of sites you can explore.

Free web-based e-mail addresses for receiving answers to queries can be obtained through most of the major Internet search sites such as Hotmail, Yahoo, and Excite. The beauty of these is that you can receive e-mail on any computer where you have Internet access, not just one that is hooked up to a specific server. Even though I'm hooked up at home to a private Internet service provider, I switched my e-mail address to one of these web-based sites for the accessibility.

If you have a question to address to a specific Pagan author, publisher, musician, artist, etc., your best chance of receiving an answer is to ask via e-mail. Contrary to popular fantasy, most artists in any genre hold down full-time jobs and, with life's other demands, have little time for letter writing. Check out a publisher's or a periodical's website for the e-mail addresses of writers and artists whose work you admire.

My e-mail address appears below. I'm always glad to hear from others who are interested in Witchcraft. I try to respond to all messages that appear in my inbox. Just be aware that sometimes my backlog of unanswered items can trail back for months.

edainmccoy@yahoo.com

If you write via snail mail to a business or to any person unknown to you, Pagan or otherwise, you should always enclose a self-addressed stamped envelope or international rely coupon. This is a matter of both courtesy and economic reality. The tally of hundreds of envelopes, sheets of paper, ink, and stamps make answering letters without return postage cost prohibitive.

To make answering easier you should word your question clearly, noting a specific page number if you are asking about a passage in a book. I get presented lots of blanket question that read like, "Tell me everything you know about Witchcraft." These types of general queries just can't be covered in a letter. They frustrate me because I wish I could do more, and it frustrates the letter writer who really wants to know or he or she wouldn't have taken the time to write. I usually reply to these with a list of books I think might help that person get started on a course of study.

For the sake of saving yourself a couple stamps, make sure your question has not already been addressed in other sources, or even in the book you're asking about. Most Pagan books contain resources appendices, bibliographies, recommended reading lists, periodical information, and glossaries in the back that can act as a springboard for the information you seek. On top of the fact that your answer may already be close at hand, a book or article on the topic you're interested in will be much more thorough and informative than a paragraph or two in any letter could be, so you will simply get a better answer.

Because I've found that I'm asked the same questions in 90 percent of the mail I receive, I'm providing those answers here for those who are interested. Hopefully this will answer many of your basic questions and help you find the other resources you seek. Best of luck, and may the Lord and Lady bless and light your pathway to their sides.

1) How do I become a Witch?

A Witch is made through study and practice. Period. By tradition it takes a year and a day of reading, working, and learning to know and love the deities you seek to connect with and worship. At this point it is acceptable to do a self-initiation and call yourself a Witch, Wiccan, or Pagan.

Initiation—self or otherwise—does not mean that the learning process has stopped. It has just begun. You've only scratched the surface of the door that opens to all worlds. To pass through it and back at will takes much more skill and effort.

Self-initiations are accepted by virtually anyone within the Pagan community as a valid expression of your commitment to the Craft.. No one will question that you're a Witch as long as you display the knowledge expected of an initiate with a year and day's study behind them. However, know that if you are interested in a particular tradition—or sect or subsect—within the Craft, you will have to be initiated into it through their priests and priestesses and their teaching structure to be considered a member within that tradition.

As previously mentioned, this is not a question that can be answered in a paragraph or two. If you are serious about being a Witch, then you can be serious about finding resources to answer you thoroughly. There are lots of good books on basic Witchcraft available, most of them with lots of practical exercises that enhance the text and cover questions in depth. Look for books by Silver RavenWolf, Scott Cunningham, Laurie Cabot, Raymond Buckland, Marion Weinstein, Vivianne Crowley, Starhawk, Gerina Dunwich, Ann Moura, and Stewart and Janet Farrar to start. If your local bookstore cannot find these authors for you, search an online bookstore or Pagan vendor such as www.amazon.com or www.azuregreen.com.

2) Where can I find a coven in my area?

This is probably the single most asked question I receive. There have been so many queries over the years that I was inspired to write *Inside a Witches' Coven* (Llewellyn, 1997) to address every nuance of the issue. The only answer to this question is that you have to hunt. No coven will ever come seeking you. Many established covens don't even want new members. The only exception to this are some teaching covens who would take you into an outer circle with other new-comers. Your best bet may be to find other solitaries and form your own group if this is the way you wish to worship.

Your search will be made much easier if you decide well ahead of time exactly what you want from a coven. Are you looking for study partners, ritual partners, magickal partners? Do you want to engage in ritual nudity, wear robes, wear street clothes? Do you want to call upon Celtic deities, German deities, only female deities? Not every coven is right for every Witch, any more than every church is right for every Christian. The wrong one can be worse than none at all.

To begin your search for a coven, look for notices of open circles or public gatherings in occult stores, metaphysical bookshops, alternative newspapers, Pagan publications, or health-food store bulletin boards. Subscribe to the Pagan publications listed in the back of virtually every book on Witchcraft and look for what is happening both around the world and around the corner.

Here's another tip for saving a stamp. Writing to a Pagan author, musician, or publisher to ask where the local covens are is useless. We often don't know where all the covens are in our hometowns, much less in places we've never been. If we did, we still would not be at liberty to invade their privacy and put them at risk by giving their personal information to others. Persistent effort on your part is the only way to ferret out the fey folk in your own area.

3) Where can I buy herbs, oils, and ritual tools?

Start by looking in your phone book under "books" for stores that sell occult books. Chances are they also sell ritual tools and magickal accoutrements.

If you live in an area without such a resource, you'll have to use mail order. I can't overstress how useful subscribing to the major Pagan publications can be in your search for absolutely anything Pagan. *Green Egg, PanGaia, SageWoman, Green Man, Hecate's Loom, Beltane Papers,* and *Circle Magazine* are all professionally formatted magazines with wide circulations in North America. Europe has many publications just as fine. Information on these can usually be found in the backs of most books on magick or Paganism, such as this one. Larger bookstores now carry several of these on their newsstands. Mail-order vendors advertise heavily in these publications, and many have online stores so you don't have to leave your living room to order a new wand. Fire up those search engines and see what you find.

4) We only have three people interested. Can we be a coven?

The answer is yes, yes, yes. Forget every movie on Witchcraft you've ever seen for right now. They got some things right . . . usually just enough to confuse everybody.

A coven is made of two or more. You don't need an individual for each element or direction. This is both limiting and silly. You don't need thirteen bodies, though this has always been touted as a traditional number. You don't need equal numbers of men and women either. How that became a requirement when those traditional thirteen people would make an unequal number of men and women has always been beyond my grasp. The Latin root *con* means "to come together" or "to be with," it specifies no number.

If you can find just one other person with whom you can work in harmony and balance and unity of vision, you are blessed. Stop worrying about trivialities that don't matter to the God and Goddess you seek to worship. Your coven of two will run smoother and work better than if you had ten people who weren't as well in tune.

5) My spells aren't working. What's wrong?

This is a hard question to answer without analyzing all elements of a spell. Even when all elements are assessed, we still may not know why a spell has failed.

First of all, make sure it has failed. Look back on your words of power and your visualization and be sure you asked for what you wanted. If you asked for a "companion" and got a dog, then your spell worked—whether you were longing for a romantic partner from it or not. This is another reason why the generic words of power found in books on spells and magick, such as this one, are not always appropriate to use exactly as they appear. They are not commandments but suggestions. You need to find those whose form and essence you feel in tune with, then hone them to your precise magickal requirements. This is not to say that they can't work just as they are, but making alterations to suit your needs and affinities will allow you to get the most out of them. If you're not going to get the most you can, why go through the effort of doing the spells in the first place?

There are only two reasons why spells fail. Either the proper effort was not put into it in the first place, or there is a stronger force opposing your spell. This opposition doesn't have to come from a concerted magickal effort. It can come from no more than the will of those involved to walk their own paths through life and not bend to the desires of anyone else. There is nothing you can do about this opposing force other than to quadruple your magickal efforts, which will likely propel you into manipulative magick to override those free wills. Even with all the redoubled efforts, you still may not be able to get what you want if the opposing force remains strong enough.

When it's your own magickal efforts that have not been enough, you have some options. First, read through that spell and all its words of power. Do some divinations. Is everything spelled out exactly the way you want it? Second, be sure you're doing more than mouthing words and making gestures. Spend time—repeatedly if necessary—doing the spell with all the energy you can project into it. Third, draw in every catalyst you can keep track of and work within the waxing and waning cycles of the moon. Gear your spell to gain on the waxing cycle and to loss on the waning cycle.

6) I want to be a Witch and learn to cast spells and curses. Where can I learn?

The first thing to learn is that Witchcraft is a religion. Worship of the God and Goddess is its primary function. Witches accept magick because we have not rejected the energies on which it is based. It works for us and that's hard evidence to refute. Yet we don't belong to the Spell of the Hour Club. Many newcomers are often surprised to learn that magick is the last subject covered when studying the Craft with a good teacher. Magick is part of our lives. It is all around us. It is us. It is not a panacea for all our problems or our first line of action for every situation we wish to change.

Because we are a religion, our actions are based on ethics. Ours teach us that we must harm none in all we do. Cursing is not a good thing, and it's a practice almost all Witches shun. To work negative magick or violate someone's free will

will rebound on us in hideous ways and is just not worth the effort. Most of us accept this and enjoy working within this bond of sacred trust with the universe without feeling restricted in any way. Adherents of all religions have their renegades, and sadly Witchcraft has a few who have to learn these lessons the hard way.

The second thing to learn is that the terms "magician" and "Witch" can be mutually exclusive. Folk magick is the inheritance of all people. Anyone can practice it, and many do with good results. If you find you hesitate to give up your current religion for magick, then don't. You can either practice folk magick or study ceremonial magick, which is an old art with Egyptian and Judeo-Christian roots that summons spirits to assist in magickal operations. If you are interested in the latter, look for books by Aleister Crowley, John Michael Greer, Donald Michael Kraig, Israel Regardie, Stephen Skinner and Francis King, and Chic and Tabatha Cicero to start you on your way.

Books on Witchcraft usually include a chapter or two on natural magick. I wrote a book about cultivating natural magickal skills called *Making Magick* (Llewellyn, 1997). There are also books on specific types of magick like herbalism, tarot, or candle. Look for books by Scott Cunningham and Raymond Buckland for beginner's guides to some of these.

7) When can I call myself a high priest/ess or elder?

This depends on your tradition if you have have aligned yourself with a specific one. Some traditions within the Craft set time frames for attaining these titles. For example, the tradition I follow deems you a priest or priestess after your initiation, and you become an elder by being part of the tradition for nine more years. Other traditions prescribe programs of study with other elders to advance. New initiations are performed to mark each rite of passage. These titles are conferred more on learning standards than time factors, though both can apply.

If you are a solitary Witch and want to attain these titles, the best course of action for you is a combination of time and continuing study. If you've been in the Craft for more than three years and work hard at learning, then you ought to consider how you view your spiritual body. Are you a leader, a mediator, a teacher, a counselor, a worker bee, an organizer, a bard? Think hard about what it is you want from your spiritual life. Then meditate on your situation to decide what is the right title for you and how to best attain it and, most importantly, live it.

8) Where can I find a Craft teacher?

There is an old magickal adage that says, "When the student is ready, the teacher will appear." But, as with any magickal goal, you can't sit at home doing nothing and expect what you wish for to knock on your door. The worthy student seeks for what he or she needs. You'll need to put the same effort into finding a teacher as you would into finding a coven. No one will hand it to you.

Thanks to Witchcraft's revival, some of the best teaching can now be found in books. Expose yourself to as many different Wiccan and Pagan ideas as you can to decide what works for you. Even if you find a teacher, you will probably find he or she wants you to read many of these books anyway, as well as lots of texts on mythology, history, science, and culture. I feel the best-educated Witches are both widely read and have worked with several teachers.

Use caution when working with a teacher. Ask for references and be sure your teacher is ethical, well-trained, and will help and not hinder your progress.

9) I need (list your need here) really fast. How can I learn to do magick right now?

You can't. It's just not that simple. If it were, everyone would be beautiful, rich, famous, and have everything they ever wanted. Magick is work. Hard work. It requires physical, emotional, and mental effort, not once, but over and over again.

Magick cannot be mastered in a day any more than other skills can. It also requires that you have a solid emotional and mental foundation on which to build. It is not to be used when nothing is going right for you. One of the most famous modern Witches, the late Sybil Leek, wrote that before making successful magick you must "see to your own house first." In other words, you need some stability and order in your life, and to have your major needs taken care of, before you can devote the kind of effort that magick requires.

If you want magick to be a part of your life, then start studying it now. Just don't do so with an eye to solving an immediate problem solely with magick. Even the mainstream religions teach that God helps those who help themselves. Be ready to back up your magick with every effort you can make to manifest your goal. Only then will it be a reality.

references

Author's Note: As is the case with many books on natural magick, this is no traditional bibliography, naming the top 100 works consulted or cited during its creation. Anyone who has practiced spellcrafting for more than a couple years—and I've been at it for nineteen years as I write these words—critically sorts knowledge to reform and combine all that has been learned with both the teachings of others and with personal experimentation born out of a developing magickal instinct. Without these elements in place, spellcrafting can never reach its peak of potency nor can it offer any spiritual satisfaction.

Please view this reference list as a mini-resource center for jumpstarting your personal exploration into magick of all kinds. Each year about 50,000 new books are published just within the United States, many on the topics of magick, spellcraft, mythology, mystery religions, romance, appearance, skin care, and cosmetics. Obviously no one will ever read everything available on these subjects, so I offer my reference list as no more than a starting point. I invite you to use it as a springboard for your own journey of magickal beauty. Read all you can. Sift out what works for you. Mentally store the rest for review later. As you sort, reform, and practice, you will develop not only your magickal skills, but your personal magickal style.

Ashe, Geoffrey. *The Virgin.* London: Routledge and Kegan Paul, 1976.

Aucoin, Kevin. *Face Forward.* Boston: Little, Brown & Co., 2000.

———. *Making Faces.* Boston: Little, Brown & Co., 1997.

Avery, Maryjean Watson, and David M. Avery. *What Is Beautiful?* Berkeley, Calif.: Tricycle Press, 1995.

Campanelli, Pauline, and Dan Campanelli. *Circles, Groves and Sanctuaries.* St. Paul, Minn.: Llewellyn Publications, 1992.

Campbell, Joseph. *The Mythic Image.* Princeton, N.J.: Princeton University Press, 1974.

———. *The Tranformation of Myth Through Time.* New York, N.Y.: Harper and Row, 1990.

Chernin, Kim. *The Obsession: Reflections on the Tyranny of Slenderness.* New York, N.Y.: Perennial Library, 1981.

———. *Sex and Other Sacred Games.* New York, N.Y.: Times Books, 1989.

Chia, Mantak, and Maneewan Chia. *Healing Love Through the Tao: Cultivating Female Sexual Energy.* Huntington, N.Y.: Healing Tao Books, 1986.

Chiazzari, Suzy. *The Complete Book of Color: Using Color for Lifestyle, Health, and Well-Being.* New York, N.Y.: Barnes and Noble, 1998.

Cunningham, Scott. *The Complete Book of Incense, Oils and Brews*. St. Paul, Minn.: Llewellyn Publications, 1989.

———. *Cunningham's Encyclopedia of Magical Herbs*. St. Paul, Minn.: Llewellyn Publications, 1986.

———. *Magical Aromatherapy: The Power of Scent*. St. Paul, Minn.: Llewellyn Publications, 1989.

Farrar, Janet, and Stewart Farrar. *The Witches' Goddess*. Custer, Wash.: Phoenix Publishing, 1987.

Frederick, Paul. *The Meaning of Aphrodite*. Chicago: The University of Chicago Press, 1978.

Gimbutas, Marija. *Goddesses and Gods of Old Europe*. Berkeley: University of California Press, 1982.

Green, Miranda J. *Symbol and Image in Celtic Religious Art*. London: Routledge, 1992.

Grigson, Geoffrey. *The Goddess of Love: The Birth, Triumph, Death and Return of Aphrodite*. New York, N.Y.: Stein and Day, 1977.

Haddon, Dayle. *Ageless Beauty*. New York, N.Y.: Hyperion Books, 1998.

Hayes, Carolyn H. *Pergemin: Perfumes, Incenses, Colors, Birthstones and Their Occult Properties and Uses*. Chicago: Aries Press, 1937.

Hoch-Smith, Judith, and Anita Spring. *Women in Ritual and Symbolic Roles*. New York, N.Y.: Plenum Press, 1978.

Keane, Patrick J. *Terrible Beauty: Yeats, Joyce, Ireland and the Myth of the Devouring Female*. Columbia, Mo.: The University of Missouri Press, 1988.

LaPuma, Karen. *Awakening Female Power*. Fairfax, Calif.: SoulSource Publishing, 1991.

Leyel, C. F. *The Magic of Herbs.* Toronto: Coles Press, 1981. Originally published 1926.

Matthews, Caitlin. *The Elements of the Goddess.* Longmeade, Shaftsbury, Dorset: Element Books, 1989.

Mariechild, Diane. *Mother Wit: A Feminist Guide to Psychic Developement.* Freedom, Calif.: The Crossing Press, 1981.

McCoy, Edain. *Celtic Women's Spirituality.* St. Paul, Minn.: Llewellyn Publications, 1998.

———. *Making Magick: What It Is and How It Works.* St. Paul, Minn.: Llewellyn Publications, 1997.

———. *A Witch's Guide to Faery Folk.* St. Paul, Minn.: Llewellyn Publications, 1994.

Millar, Elisabeth. *The Fragrant Veil: Scents for the Sensuous Woman.* St. Paul, Minn.: Llewellyn Publications, 2000.

Miller, Richard Alan, and Iona Miller. *The Magical and Ritual Use of Perfumes.* Rochester, Vt.: Destiny Books, 1990.

Monaghan, Patricia. *Magical Gardens.* St. Paul, Minn.: Llewellyn Publications, 1997.

———. *The New Book of Goddesses & Heroines.* Third Edition. St. Paul, Minn.: Llewellyn Publications, 1997.

Paulsen, Kathryn. *Witches' Potions and Spells.* Mount Vernon, N.Y.: Peter Pauper Press, 1971.

Rose, Jeanne. *Herbal Body Book.* Berkeley, Calif.: Frog, Ltd., 2000.

Sabrina, Lady. *Reclaiming the Power.* St. Paul, Minn.: Llewellyn Publications, 1992.

Sherrow, Victoria. *For Appearances Sake.* Phoenix: Oryx Press, 2000.

Shuttle, Penelope, and Peter Redgrove. *The Wise Wound: Myths, Realities and Meanings of Menstruation* (revised). New York, N.Y.: Bantam Books, 1990. Original edition published 1978.

Telesco, Patricia. *A Kitchen Witch's Cookbook.* St. Paul, Minn.: Llewellyn Publications, 1994.

Walker, Barbara G. *The Crone: Woman of Age, Wisdom and Power.* San Francisco: HarperCollins, 1990.

Weiss, Stephanie Iris. *Coping with the Beauty Myth* (Coping Series for Young Adults). Reading, Mass.: Rosen Publishing, 2000.

Williams, Selma R. *Riding the Nightmare: Women and Witchcraft from the Old World to Colonial Salem.* San Francisco: HarperPerrenial, 1992.

Wolf, Naomi. *The Beauty Myth: How Images of Beauty Are Used Against Women.* New York, N.Y.: Anchor, 1992.

index

212

Bewitchments
Love Magick for Modern Romance

EDAIN McCOY

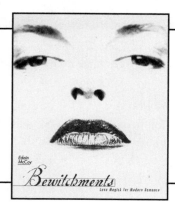

The simple act of braiding your hair can be a potent spell for love—that's why Celtic women had to wear their hair loose at their weddings. Eat a pineapple, long a symbol of friendship and unity, and watch new friends come into your life. Whether you're looking for a new friend or a lifelong mate, *Bewitchments* can help you narrow the focus of the search and show you how to attract, sustain, or refine these relationships with its grimoire of over ninety spells. Drawing on both multicultural folk magick and new scientific discoveries about the chemical process known as "falling in love," *Bewitchments* shows, step by step, how to bring the ancient spells into the present and make them work.

1-56718-700-5
264 pp., 7½ x 9⅛, illus. $14.95